LIVING PASSIONATELY FC

CAS MONACO

LIVING PASSIONATELY
FOR CHRIST

A devotional Bible study
on the book of Philippians

Entrusting God's Treasure
To The Faithful

1st printing, August 2003

All Scripture
New American Standard Bible
Reference Edition,
LaHabra: A.J. Holman Company, 1960.

To the university students involved in the
Portland Metro Ministry who help to keep my passion alive.

CONTENTS

ACKNOWLEDGEMENTS

Thank you to the students in my Tuesday Bible study, and Bincy, Cara, Janean, Karen and Kristi for helping me every step of the way. Thank you Tyler and Amy—without your design expertise and sacrificial service I'd be lost.

LIVING PASSIONATELY FOR CHRIST

What are you passionate about? What is it that makes you pound your fist with conviction? What occupies your mind and compels you to action? Passion and zeal aren't lacking in our world today. Consider the intensity with which men and women strive to beat a world's record, to be the first to brave the frozen wastelands of the Antarctica, or to conquer the treacherous cliffs of Mount Everest—risking their lives to accomplish an earthly goal. Even more extreme are the young men and women whose religious beliefs and deep-seated hatred compel them to become human bombs—blowing up themselves and others. They blindly believe that a martyr's death is most pleasing to their god and guarantees passage to paradise. The pinnacle of vehement passion slammed onto our television screens, into headlines, and across the radio waves on September 11, 2002. These horrific events changed the face of America and the world in a matter of minutes.

The call to Christ-centered living resonates throughout the New Testament.

The intensity with which non-believers live and die for their cause should stop us—children of God—dead in our tracks. To what are we devoting our lives? Is Jesus Christ really at the center of our every life decision, or is His name tacked onto our life's resume to prove we're in good standing before God, giving us clearance to live our lives the way we want to? Are we willing to settle for the "middle-of-the-road" in our walk and service for the Lord? If anyone has reason to live with intense, joy-filled, purposeful passion, it is the Christian who holds the only answer to the world's problems—the Lord Jesus Christ. Do we really believe this? Are we living and breathing and responding to the life to which God has called us? These are questions I ask myself over and over again and questions believers ought to repeatedly ask themselves as well. These are questions that compel me to "raise the bar" in my own life, and prayerfully in yours as well.

The call to Christ-centered living resonates throughout the New Testament. Particularly in the book of Philippians the challenge rings loud and clear. The apostle Paul expresses his loyal and fervent commitment to live and to willingly die for the glory of Jesus Christ. We perceive Paul's passionate love for the Lord through his heart for the lost, his call to Christ-centered living, and his goal to live in light of eternity. The fact that he is writing this letter from inside walls emphasizes Paul's unwavering zeal. As we study Philippians, we will ascertain the source of and the reason for passionate, Christ-centered living. We will discover what sets a believer apart, how such a believer will make an impact on the world—through relationships with family and friends, in the workplace, in sickness and through affliction. We will stretch the limits of our faith for the glory of God, as we say: "**...I count all things as loss in view of the surpassing value of knowing Christ Jesus...**" (Philippians 3:7). Whether you're a brand-new believer or one who has followed Christ for a long time, digging deeply into the treasure-chest of God's Word will lead you to the only One worth living for—the Lord Jesus Christ.

"Now Saul, still breathing threats and murder against the disciples of the Lord..."

Acts 9:1

"For to me, to live is Christ, and to die is gain."

Philippians 1:21

Transformed Passion

DAY ONE

☐ Read Philippians

Jesus Christ changes lives!—Acts 6-7

Our study begins with Stephen standing before a council of Jewish extremists called the "Synagogue of the Freedmen"—led by Saul—who were intent upon destroying the followers of Jesus Christ. These men stirred up the people and found false witnesses who accused Stephen of blasphemy and "incessantly speaking against this holy place, and the Law; hearing him say that this Nazarene, Jesus, will destroy this place and alter the customs which Moses handed down to us" (Acts 6:13-14). As Stephen stood on trial before this hostile council his face was described as being like "the face of an angel" (Acts 6:15).

1. a. Read Acts 7. Briefly describe Stephen's defense and the end result.

    b. According to Acts 7:54-58, how did the men react to the name of the Lord Jesus Christ, and why?

2. a. What does Acts 7:60 reveal about Stephen's character?

b. What do you learn about passion and conviction from Stephen's life and death?

Reflection

Stephen's courageous faith is inspiring. In the face of an angry mob he proclaimed with boldness the gospel—risking his life for Jesus Christ. Thank the Lord for Stephen's example, and pray that the Lord will give you strength and courage to live the Christian life with confidence.

DAY TWO

☐ Read Philippians

The man Saul—Acts 7-9

Devotion, prayer, miracles, signs, wonders, power, and boldness—all words that aptly described the early church; however, don't miss the fact that ravaging, persecution, hatred, and murder defined the times as well. A brief account of Stephen's life ends at the feet of a young leader named Saul whose zeal and murderous threats were well known by believers and non-believers alike.

3. TRUTH SEARCH:

   a. Look at Acts 7:58, Acts 8:1-3, and Acts 9:1-2 and record the words that describe the man Saul.

   b. How does his passion compare with Stephen's?

4. a. Look closely at Acts 9:3-9 and describe in your own words what happened on the road to Damascus.

b. Who was Saul really persecuting?

5. a. What does the Lord ask of Ananias in Acts 9:10-14, and what was his initial response?

    b. Read Acts 9:15-29. What changes begin taking place in Saul's life? Keep your eyes on the text.

Reflection

Later in Acts 13 we learn that the Lord changed Saul's name to Paul. The once murderous persecutor of Christ and His followers becomes the man God uses to pen most of the New Testament, the man who writes "for me to live is Christ and to die is gain." Jesus Christ transforms lives!

Praise the Lord for the power of His forgiveness! Praise Him for saving you and transforming your heart and life. Perhaps you've been praying for someone who, like Saul, is hostile toward the gospel. Thank the Lord for the example of His mercy and grace demonstrated in Paul's life and your own, and trust Him with renewed faith.

DAY THREE

☐ Read Philippians

@ DIGGING DEEPER

Acts 1-9 gives us a brief survey of the mighty power of God's Spirit at work in the hearts and lives of men and women in the days and weeks after Jesus ascended into heaven. God's Spirit is still working with the same transforming power in our lives today. Spend time meditating on the following passages of scripture that describe the transformation that begins in our lives the moment we place our faith in Christ.

6.   Record all of the changes that have taken place in your life because of Jesus Christ. Praise and thank Him for your discoveries.

Example: Philippians 1:6 "For I am confident of this very thing, that He who began a good work in you will perfect it until the day of Christ Jesus." I can rest in the fact that the Lord is the One who began our relationship. He began a "good work" in my heart and life, and from now until the day I step into heaven, He is working in me to make me more like Him.

   II Corinthians 5:17

   Galatians 2:20

   Ephesians 2:8-10

   Ephesians 4:20-24

   Colossians 2:6-7, 10, 13-14

Reflection

Each of these passages describes in simple yet profound detail the remarkable changes Jesus Christ makes in our hearts and our lives. Whether we're old or young in Christ, these truths describe our faith and walk with the Lord Jesus Christ. May we never tire of these truths and may they ever motivate us to live our lives wholeheartedly for Him.

⌒ Study Tools

I've been walking with the Lord for over twenty years and the one thing I continue to learn is the importance of being in the Word and spending time with the Lord—the need to do so never changes and perhaps even increases the older I get! The following are some practical suggestions—things I have incorporated into my life that have helped me along the path of life.

- Make your time with the Lord a *non-negotiable* part of your life. You eat and sleep every-day, right? Schedule in daily time with the Lord. Maybe it needs to be the first thing you do before your day begins. Get up fifteen, thirty, sixty minutes early. If you're a student, schedule time during one of your free hours during the day, if you work use your lunch hour. For some the best time is at night—regardless when is best for you, make it *non-negotiable*.

- Read five Psalms a day along with one chapter of Proverbs. If you follow this pattern you'll read through the books of Psalms and Proverbs once a month.

- This study is designed to help you spend time with the Lord and in His Word at least five times a week. Additionally, this study suggests that you read Philippians everyday. As a young believer I learned to read whatever book of the Bible I'm studying all the way through 50 times. I have found this to be an invaluable tool of study. I not only learn the book, but I also nearly memorize it! If you read Philippians as indicated in this study you'll have read it 50 times by the time you finish.

DAY FOUR

☐ Read Philippians

The power of a transformed life—Acts 16:6-40

Paul was transformed from a ravenous persecutor of Jesus Christ and His followers to a passionate witness and follower of Jesus Christ. Acts 16:6-40 focuses in on the supernatural way in which the Lord worked through the now apostle Paul and his co-laborers to preach the gospel in the city of Philippi.

7.   a. Read Acts 16:6-9. How did the Lord guide and direct Paul and his disciples?

      b. Look carefully at Acts 16:10. How did they respond to God's leading?

      c. Recently a friend of mine pointed out that as a result of Paul's sensitivity to the Holy Spirit's leading and his immediate obedience, the gospel traveled from the Middle East to modern day Western Europe. Are you willing to follow the Lord wherever He leads, even if it means a drastic change of course?

8. a. Read Acts 16:11-15 and record what you learn about Philippi and Paul's initial discoveries. Keep your eyes on the text.

    b. Briefly describe your own surroundings. Consider people's religious beliefs, and political perspective. How do these affect your walk and your witness?

9. a. Where is the first place Paul and Silas go, and what happens in Lydia's life?

    b. What happens in her family as a result (Acts 16:15)?

10. Read Acts 16:16-24. Describe the events leading up to Paul and Silas' imprisonment.

11. a. Look closely at Acts 16:25-34. How would you describe Paul and Silas' attitude toward their imprisonment? What does this teach you about their character and perspective?

    b. Had Paul and Silas been looking at their circumstances and not the Lord, how might they have reacted to these events?

12. In this same passage describe what happens not only to Paul and Silas, but to all the prisoners, the jailer, and his household.

Reflection

"O Lord, Thou hast searched me and known me.

Thou dost know when I sit down and when I rise up.

Thou dost understand my thought from afar.

Thou dost scrutinize my path and my lying down,

And art intimately acquainted with all my ways."

—Psalm 139:1-3

Whether chaotic or mundane, every event is being orchestrated by the Lord to fulfill His divine purpose for our lives. As the Psalmist says, "He is *intimately* acquainted with all our ways." Consider your own life and the circumstances you're facing right now. What have you learned about God's purpose for your life from your study today?

DAY FIVE

☐ Read Philippians

Real Life

God's Word is applicable in every aspect of our lives. Today we will spend time considering the practical application of the passages we have looked at this week. Pray that the Lord will give you wisdom as you study and as you seek to live out these truths in your day to day life.

13. a. What differences do you observe in Paul's life before and after his conversion?

   b. What does this teach you, personally, about the grace of God?

14. Briefly describe your spiritual journey. How did you come to know Jesus Christ personally? List two or three of the most significant changes He has made in your life.

15. Two of the people who became Christians in this chapter where Lydia and the jailer. What are the differences between these conversions, and what does this teach you about evangelism?

16. Is there someone with whom you have been sharing the Gospel? How do these different conversion experiences encourage you as you talk with unbelievers?

Perhaps the Lord has you in what humanly speaking is a very unlikely place to share the gospel. Or maybe there is someone in your life like Lydia who knows the things of God but has never known Him as Savior. Could it be that the Lord is going to use your life for His glory in this situation? Thank Him for changing your life and for using you in the lives of others. Watch for opportunities to be used by Him every day this week!

17. Describe the ways in which you have seen the Lord transforming your life and heart over the past few weeks and months. How do the passages you've studied specifically encourage or challenge you in the process?

Reflection

Our study began with Stephen standing before the Council of the Jews, demonstrating passionate devotion to Jesus Christ and ultimately giving his life for the gospel. We watched as Saul was transformed from being a ravenous persecutor of Christians to a zealous child of God. Only God can change a person from the inside out—what a privilege to know Him! Pray that the Lord will help you grasp the transforming truths of His Word in your life this week. Pray that you will find yourself following Him with passionate devotion, growing closer to Him and overflowing with His love.

"For I am confident of this very thing, that He who began a good work in you will perfect it until the day of Christ Jesus."

Philippians 1:6

Transformed Confidence

Philippians 1:1-11

In elementary school I remember peering into an old mayonnaise jar in which sat a cocoon attached to a short stick. We were studying about how a caterpillar—neon green, squishy, and hairy—would weave a thick, wool-like blanket in which to hide himself for a period of several weeks. For what seemed like decades we watched the cocoon sitting there, never moving, never changing color, never doing anything interesting at all. Then one day we noticed a little slit along the edge of the caterpillar's blanket. It didn't take long before we could see long, skinny, black tendrils working feverishly—the slit growing into a gap—and eventually a black, bug head emerged from the darkness of the cocoon. The creature, in no way resembling a caterpillar, pulled itself out of the hole. Struggling as if to gain balance on the slender twig, it unfurled two beautifully colored wings and revealed its new identity—a delicate, colorful butterfly. It was an incredible, mind boggling sight. How could such absolute change take place without any apparent effort? Impossible without the Creator God!

Metamorphosis means "a marked or complete change of character, appearance, condition."

Metamorphosis means "a marked or complete change of character, appearance, condition."[1] As we read about Saul's conversion in the book of Acts we 'watched' a spiritual metamorphosis take place. Saul's life was transformed when he met Jesus Christ face to face. Not only did the Lord change his name to Paul, but He also changed his character—completely and permanently—by the power of His Holy Spirit. That same transformation occurred in our lives as well. The very moment we placed our faith in Jesus Christ, you and I became new creations, our identities changed, and we became children of God. This transformation is complete and permanent; our *position in Christ* is absolutely secure. Yet the transformation is ongoing as we learn to walk in the power of the Holy Spirit and to obey God's Word. Philippians has been called the book of Christian experience because of its practical application. Throughout all four chapters we learn about the security of our *position in Christ* and how it affects our choices, relationships, and purpose. In Philippians we learn how to live out the truths of God's Word in our everyday experience.

As you begin your study of the Word today pray for an undistracted heart. Pray that the truths of your position in Christ will make sense, and that your confidence will grow as you understand more about the transformation that has taken place in your life. If these truths are familiar to you, ask the Lord to refresh your heart, to make them new again to you. Thank Him for His Word and the power of His Spirit.

DAY ONE

☐ Read Philippians

Partnership & Confidence—Philippians 1:1-5

Paul's first visit to Philippi, as you will recall, was wild! Acts 16:9 tells us, "And a vision appeared to Paul in the night: a certain man of Macedonia was standing and appealing to him, and saying, 'Come over to Macedonia and help us.' And when he had seen the vision, immediately we sought to go into Macedonia, concluding that God had called us to preach the gospel to them." Obeying the Lord, Paul and his men went to Philippi where they met and spoke to Lydia. The Lord opened her heart and she became a believer in Jesus Christ. They were beaten and thrown into jail because they were "throwing the city into confusion" (Acts 16:20). While in jail they experienced a great earthquake that caused everyone's chains to fall off. The guard, fearing that all the prisoners would escape and he'd be to blame, nearly killed himself. Paul stopped him and led him and his family to salvation in Christ.

Though Paul only visited Philippi one more time, he obviously felt a fond affection and closeness toward the believers there and cared deeply about their spiritual growth and health. He knew from experience the opposition they faced as followers of Jesus Christ. We not only learn about his care for this church, but also his passion for Jesus Christ.

1. Read through all four chapters of Philippians. What do the following passages tell you about Paul's passion in life? Philippians 1:18-21; 2:1-5; 3:7-11; 4:11-13.

2. What do you learn about the Lord Jesus? Look closely at Philippians 2:5-11; 3:20-21; 4:7,13,19.

3. Carefully observe each chapter and record the main idea in each chapter. Look for repeated words, like *joy*, repeated subjects like *the gospel* (don't worry about getting the "right" answer—just make observations).

ᴄ— STUDY TOOLS: DOULOS

Paul begins his letter by introducing himself and Timothy as "bond-servants of Christ Jesus" (New American Standard—NASB). "Bond-servants translates the plural of the oft-used Greek word *doulos*, which describes a person owned by someone else and thus subservient to and dependent on that person. When used in the New Testament of a believer's relationship to Jesus Christ, *doulos* describes willing, determined, and devoted service. It reflects the attitude of an Old Testament slave who refused the opportunity for freedom and voluntarily resubmitted himself to his master for life. In that spirit Paul and Timothy did not think of being bond-servants of Christ Jesus in anything but positive terms. Nor did they think of themselves as bondservants of the church, of Rome, or of any other person or institution, but exclusively of Christ Jesus."[2].

---

4. a. Look at Philippians 1:3-5. What brings Paul joy as he remembers the Philippians?

b. What does it mean to participate or partner in the gospel with someone or a group of people?

c. Is there someone in your life who is participating in the ministry with you? What is it that you see in his/her walk with the Lord that you're thankful for?

Reflection

Think about what it means for you to be Jesus Christ's *bondservant*—His *willing, determined, and devoted slave*? Thank Him for being an all-loving, forgiving, powerful, holy, righteous Master. Thank Him for calling you to be His willing slave.

DAY TWO

☐ Read Philippians

Confidence in Christ - Philippians 1:6

Paul is a great example of one whose life was transformed by Jesus Christ. Outwardly his words and actions were turned upside-down! Inwardly his heart softened toward the Lord, and his pride and arrogance turned into humility and kindness, and he had a newfound confidence—a confidence *in Christ*. Not only had this good work begun in Paul's life, but it also had begun in the lives of the believers in Philippi. It began in our lives as well—the very moment we placed our faith in Christ.

5. a. Write out the encouraging promise found in Philippians 1:6.

      b. Define <u>confidence:</u>

6. In whom does Paul place his confidence and how does this differ from before he came to know Christ as his Savior (see Philippians 3:3-7 for insight)?

7.   TRUTH SEARCH

a. Look up the following verses and record what you learn about your confidence *in Christ*: II Corinthians 3:4-6; Ephesians 3:11-12 and Hebrews 4:14-16; Hebrews 13:6; I John 4:15-18.

b. Which of these verses encourages you the most, and why?

Reflection

Jesus Christ is the centerpiece of our confidence. Because of all that Jesus did for us, we are adequate and we can stand boldly before Him in prayer. We are confident in any situation because He is our Helper. We have nothing to fear on the day of judgment because He is our Savior. Praise Him for the security of your relationship with Him. Pray you will grow in your confidence in Christ.

DAY THREE

☐ Read Philippians

@ DIGGING DEEPER

In today's lesson we are going to dig deeper into God's Word regarding the "good work" He began and will complete in our lives upon His return. The truths you are about to study are rich and so important. Pray that the Lord will help you understand and apply these in your heart and life.

8. To best understand our *position in Christ* we will first look at God's assessment of our condition prior to knowing Christ as our Savior. Read the list of verses and passages and record the words that describe where you stood apart from Jesus Christ.

a. Romans 3:23

b. Romans 5:6,8,10

c. Ephesians 2:1-3

d. Ephesians 2:12

The following verses and passages describe your *position in Christ*—that which is true about you because of what Jesus Christ did on the cross. The moment you placed your faith in Christ all of these changes took place in your life. Keep in mind that I'm making only a partial list of all that is true of us *in Christ*!

9. Read each verse or passage and record what is true of you because you are <u>in Christ</u> (watch for this phrase as you read):

a. Ephesians 1:3

b. Ephesians 1:4

c. Ephesians 1:5-6

d. Ephesians 1:7-8a

    e. Ephesians 1:8b-10b

    f. Ephesians 1:10c-12

    g. Ephesians 1:13

    h. Ephesians 2:10

    i. Ephesians 3:16-19

10. How can these truths boost your confidence on a practical level?

Reflection

Contemplate the transformation that has taken place in your life personally. Go back over today's lesson and read each verse or passage aloud. Praise Him for everything that is true of you because you are *in Christ Jesus*. Rejoice in your salvation!

DAY FOUR

☐ Read Philippians

Heartfelt Prayer—Philippians 1:7-11

Paul was a prayer warrior. It is evident in all of his epistles that he spent much time interceding for the many believers he was in contact with—in fact, he even said that he "prayed without ceasing"! We learn from Paul's example that prayer is of the utmost importance in our relationship with the Lord and our ministry in each other's lives. Paul prayed with an attitude of thanksgiving, joy, and faith—a reflection of his deep commitment to Jesus Christ. In Philippians 1:3-4 we learn that he was "always offering prayer with joy in his every prayer" for the believers in Philippi, and in Philippians 1:9-11 he details for us the specific things for which he prayed.

11. Look specifically at Philippians 1:7-8. What do these two verses tell you about Paul's relationship with the Philippian believers?

Philippians 1:9-11 lists the following five areas for which Paul prayed: a growing and deepening love, a pursuit of excellence, an attitude of integrity, fruitful ministry, and a life that glorified God.[3]

12. In Philippians 1:9 Paul prays that their love would abound still more and more in real knowledge and all discernment. Compare this with I Corinthians 13:1-8. Why must love and knowledge be joined together?

13. a. With the following verses in mind, explain why Paul prays for an abundance of love: John 13:34-35; I John 4:7-11.

b. Why is sacrificial love evidence of the good work Jesus began in our lives?

14. a. God's Word is the source of real knowledge and all discernment. Look at the following verses and record what you learn about the effect knowing the truth has in our lives: Romans 15:14, Ephesians 5:8-9, I Peter 1:22, Hebrews 4:12.

b. What does I Thessalonians 5:21-22 teach you about discernment?

15. a. Why are we called to "approve the things that are excellent?"

b. Examine Romans 12:2 and Philippians 4:8. What does this look like on a practical basis?

16. TRUTH SEARCH

Read Psalm 15 and describe <u>integrity</u>. How does this compare with being sincere and blameless?

b. Compare Philippians 1:10 with Psalm 15. Why are we called to live sincere and blameless lives?

17. a. With what are we filled according to Philippians 1:11, and for what purpose?

b. What is the "fruit of righteousness" (use scripture to support your answer)?

18. How will an abundance of love, a life of excellence and integrity, and a fruitful life bring glory and praise to God?

Reflection

Scripture always gives us the perfect pattern for prayer. Finish your time in God's Word today by praying through Philippians 1:7-11 for yourself, your husband, your children, your friends, and for those with whom you "participate in the gospel." Pray that their lives and yours will give glory and honor to our Lord and Savior.

DAY FIVE

☐ Read Philippians

Real Life

Ephesians 3:16-19 is another of Paul's great prayers, and contains a significant promise regarding transformed confidence: we have been granted the power of God's Holy Spirit to strengthen us and enable us to live in such a way that glorifies God. Apart from the Holy Spirit, apart from abiding in Christ and His Word, we are powerless and fruitless—and the Lord knows that. II Peter 1:3-4 says, "His divine power has granted to us everything pertaining to life and godliness, through the true knowledge of Him who called us by His own glory and excellence. For by these He has granted to us His precious and magnificent promises, in order that by them you might become partakers of the divine nature, having escaped the corruption that is in the world by lust." His divine power transformed our hearts and reconciled us to God at the point of salvation. Our position *in Christ* guarantees our forgiveness, says we're brand-new creatures, and secures our eternal life. When in doubt we can turn to the Word of God—His precious and magnificent promises—for reassurance and the power to live obediently.

19. How does your position *in Christ* make a difference in how you live your life? Consider some or all of the following as you answer: think about the things that discourage you or make you fearful and anxious. What difference can it make in your life to know that, without exception, Jesus Christ loves you absolutely and fully no matter what, and has forgiven all of your sins? How does it affect your life to know that He has blessed you, adopted you, brought you near, and grants you free access to Him twenty-four hours a day?

20. a. In what areas of your life and ministry are you tempted to lose confidence, and why?

b. What should you do when you lose your confidence in Christ?

21. a. In what area of your life are you in need of God's love and wisdom?

b. Based upon what you've learned today, Who can meet your need, and how?

Reflection

Our position in Christ is secure; we're loved, forgiven, cared about, never alone, and we could go on. However, if we're not filling our hearts and minds with the truth of God's Word regularly, we quickly fall back into relying on our flesh and seeking confidence in our performance, our position, our outward abilities or beauty. It doesn't take long before we experience stress and anxiety, and we feel like failures—unlovable and unworthy. Pray that the Lord will draw you to Himself, that He will give you the discipline to spend time in the Word and at His feet even when you don't want to. Pray that the truths of your position in Christ will radically affect your behavior and your choices, and that your goal in life will be to glorify Him.

Copy Philippians 1:1-11 in the back of your book or in your journal.

1 Webster, pg. 893
2 MacArthur, pg. 13
3 Ibid

"...that I shall not be put to shame in anything, but that with all boldness, Christ shall even now, as always, be exalted in my body, whether by life or by death."

Philippians 1:20

Transformed Purpose

Philippians 1:12-30

The apostle Paul's passion and confidence were radically changed upon surrendering his life to

Jesus Christ. He became a man who lived in light of his position in Christ. He found confidence in the fact that he'd been bought with a price, that he was forgiven, and that he possessed the hope of eternal life—all because of what Jesus Christ, his Savior, did for him. The result of his transformed passion and confidence was a newfound purpose. From the Philippian jail in Acts 16 all the way to the Roman imprisonment in Acts 28, Paul's purpose was to proclaim the good news of Jesus Christ. In spite of jealousy, idolatry, wickedness, beatings, false accusations, and threats from Jew and Gentile alike, Paul and his men were intent upon fulfilling this purpose. In Acts 17 we read of the Jews in Thessalonica who formed a mob and shouted, "These men who have upset the world have come here also…and they stirred up the crowd and the city authorities who heard these things" (Acts 17:6&8). Paul and his men left Thessalonica and went to Berea, where they took the gospel to the Jewish synagogue. The Jews "received the word with great eagerness, examining the Scriptures daily, to see whether these things were so. Many of them therefore believed, along with a number of prominent Greek women and men" (Acts 17:11-12). He and his companions went from Berea to Athens, where they reasoned "in the synagogues with Jews and God-fearing Gentiles, and in the market place every day with those who happened to be present" (Acts 17:17). From there they moved into Corinth where they stayed many months because of the number of people who were coming to Christ. Then in Ephesus they performed "extraordinary miracles" (Acts 19:11). Throughout his ministry, Paul faced both angry mobs who were intent upon taking his life, and men and women who responded to the truth and were saved from their sin. Many became devout followers of Christ and churches started in every city as a result of Paul's obedience. His perseverance and perspective compel me in my ministry. No matter how people responded, he pressed on with eager purposefulness.

Paul faced both angry mobs who were intent upon taking his life, and men and women who responded to the truth and were saved from their sin.

In Acts 21, just before Paul boarded a ship for Jerusalem, "a certain prophet named Agabus came down from Judea. And coming to us, he took Paul's belt and bound his own feet and hands, and said, 'This is what the Holy Spirit says: "In this way the Jews at Jerusalem will bind the man who owns this belt and deliver him into the hands of the Gentiles."'" And just as Agabus foretold, seven days after arriving in Jerusalem, Paul was mobbed in the temple. "And all the city was aroused, and the people rushed together; and taking hold of Paul, they dragged him out of the temple; and immediately the doors were shut. And while they were seeking to kill him, a report came up to the commander of the Roman cohort that all Jerusalem was in confusion" (Acts 21:30-31). Even after being beaten nearly to death, Paul begged the commander, who recognized that Paul had done nothing to merit imprisonment, to allow him to speak before taking him to prison. After reading this section of Acts, I had to stop and consider what I'd just "witnessed." This man's passion, purpose, and confidence centered solely and completely on his Savior. I am inspired by Paul's fearless commitment to the Lord and to the proclamation of the truth.

From the Jerusalem prison Paul was put on trial before the Council of the Jews, Governor Felix, and a Jewish attorney named Tertullus. After waiting two years for a decision regarding his case, he stood trial before a new governor named Festus. In Acts 25:11 Paul appeals as a Roman citizen to Caesar: "If then I am a wrongdoer, and have committed anything worthy of death, I do not refuse to die; but if none of those things is true of which these men accuse me, no one can hand me over the them [the Jews]. I appeal to Caesar." Festus agreed to send Paul to Rome, which did not happen until after Paul stood before King Agrippa. Again, the apostle had opportunity to witness to another man in authority. In fact, Acts 26:28 says that Agrippa was almost persuaded to become a Christian. The Lord used Paul's circumstances for the furtherance of the message of Jesus Christ.

Paul then set sail for Rome in an Adramyttian ship along with some other prisoners. Acts 27 records the treacherous journey in remarkable detail. For fourteen days these men braved a violent storm, nearly starved, and faced imminent death. Paul's faith in God strengthened these men and helped them persevere and survive. In Acts 27:34-37 Paul said, "'Therefore I encourage you to take some food, for this is for your preservation; for not a hair from the head of any of you shall perish.' And having said this, he took bread and gave thanks to God in the presence of all; and he broke it and began to eat. And all of them were encouraged, and they themselves also took food. And all of us in the ship were two hundred and seventy-six persons." Not long after lightening the ship by throwing all of their food overboard, they saw land. In Acts 27:44 we read that "all were brought safely to land." They had finally landed on the island of Malta—all 276 of them—just as Paul had promised. Paul and these men spent three months with the natives, sharing the gospel and performing miracles. What an amazing life! None of Paul's circumstances were mere coincidence. The Lord used each and every one for His purpose and His glory.

Yes, Paul finally made it to Rome where he was chained to a guard for two more years. "….they [the leading men of the Jews] came to him in large numbers; and he was explaining to them by solemnly testifying about the kingdom of God, and trying to persuade them concerning Jesus, from both the Law of Moses and from the Prophets, from morning until evening…. And he stayed two full years in his own rented quarters, and was welcoming all who came to him, preaching the kingdom of God, and teaching concerning the Lord Jesus Christ with all openness and unhindered"(Acts 28:23, 30-31).

Even though Paul was shackled, the gospel was not. The Lord not only used his imprisonment to further the gospel, but also inspired this man of God to pen most of the New Testament. May we learn from his example as we continue our study of Philippians. Pray that the Lord will use this passage of Philippians to inspire you in your circumstances. Thank Him for the place He has you—whether you're fulfilled and encouraged, or wondering how He could ever use you or your situation for His glory. Pray for His wisdom as you begin.

DAY ONE

☐ Read Philippians

Passion for the Gospel—Philippians 1:12-18

The Roman government arrested Paul because of his bold, unwavering proclamation of the gospel. Though he did not actually live inside a prison he was chained to Roman guards 24 hours a day, considered under "house arrest." From a human perspective, Paul's imprisonment was unjust and undeserved. From a heavenly perspective, his chains provided innumerable opportunities to tell all sorts of people about the Savior. We also learn that Paul's desire was to exalt Christ—to honor His name through his attitudes and actions.

1. Paul recognizes that he is imprisoned not for any wrongdoing, but for the "cause of Christ." Read Philippians 1:12-14 and describe Paul's attitude toward his circumstances. Keep your eyes on the text.

2. According to Philippians 1:13 and 4:22, with whom had Paul been able to share the gospel, and why is this significant?

3. How had Paul's imprisonment affected most of the believers in Philippi (Philippians I:14-16)?

4. According to Philippians 1:15-18, some preached the gospel from envy and strife—hoping to cause Paul distress, but all that really mattered to him was that Christ was proclaimed. What ultimately brought Paul joy, and why?

5. TRUTH SEARCH

    a. Joy is one of the main themes of Philippians. Look up the following verses and record the things that caused Paul to rejoice:
    Philippians 2:2

    Philippians 2:14-18

    Philippians 2:25-30

    Philippians 3:1, 4:4

    b. What hinders you from experiencing joy in your walk with the Lord?

    c. What choices do you need to make in order for your life to be characterized by joy?

⌒ STUDY TOOLS: THE WORD STUDY PROCESS

As a new believer I was challenged to seek the Lord with all of my heart, soul, mind and strength. Early on, the woman who was discipling me taught me how to seek the Lord by showing me how to do a word study. The first word I studied was "seek," and it proved to be very insightful and encouraging to me in my pursuit of the Lord.

1. Select a word: When observing a text, select the individual words that are the most significant to the passage's meaning or that appear interesting.

2. Look it up in a concordance: Locate the word in the main body of the concordance, taking note of the reference number. Locate the "original word" (the actual Hebrew, Aramaic, or Greek word) in the correct dictionary in the back (1. Hebrew/Aramaic or 2. Greek). Write down the definition assigned to the word, and take note of the various ways in which the word has been translated in English and which translation is most common. Note: The concordance should match the version of the Bible used.

3. Examine the original word used in other texts: Look up other passages that use this same "original word" (same reference number), even though it may be translated differently in English. This can be done by looking up the various English translations of the "original word" in the main body of the concordance and noting those passages which have the same reference number. Develop an understanding of how the "original word" (same reference number) is used in these other contexts.

4. Consult word study tools: Look up your word in a variety of study tools.

    A. Bible Dictionaries present immediate access to much scholarly information for everything "from A to Z." Look up the selected English word, and/or its synonyms if needed, and search out additional information. Note the transliteration of the second word when referenced. Revell's concise Bible Dictionary, Holman Bible Dictionary.

    B. Expository Dictionaries show how particular "original words" are translated in English, how they are used in different contexts, what theological ideas are possibly attached to a particular word, and Greek synonyms of each word. By using a combination of the selected English word (or synonym if needed), the translation of the "original word," and/or reference number, locate the transliterated "original word" and its defined usage. Vine's Expository Dictionary of Old and New Testament Words, The Complete Word Study Dictionary—OT and NT.

5. Write a summary of findings: Go back to the original passage and, based upon the general usage of the word, define the word in the light of the immediate context. Write a summary statement of the meaning of the word in this particular context. Remember, CONTEXT IS KING!

Reflection

Joy is a fruit of the Spirit-filled life and is obtained and maintained by keeping our hearts focused on Jesus Christ—not our feelings or circumstances. Psalm 16:11 says, "In His presence is fulness of joy; at His right hand there are pleasures forever." If your life lacks joy and gladness, pursue Him by spending time in His presence. Resist the urge to treat your study of Philippians as merely an intellectual exercise that you need to hurry and finish; rather make it a point to practice His presence as you read each chapter and complete each lesson. The result will be fulness of joy. If you're particularly "joyless" today, do a word study on *joy*.

DAY TWO

☐ Read Philippians

Christ Exalted—Philippians 1:19-26

Even though God used him in prison, Paul still desired to be delivered from his chains. It comforts me to know that Paul recognized his need for prayer and the deliverance of the Holy Spirit—he was just as human and weak as I am. Not merely comforted, I am also challenged by Paul's example. He didn't know if God would deliver him, yet his ultimate desire was to exalt Christ in his body—whether by life or by death. I ask myself, "do I desire that Christ be exalted, honored, glorified in my life regardless of my predicaments?" Pray with me that Jesus will teach us how to glorify Him in and through our lives no matter the situation.

6. Read Philippians 1:19-21. Paul earnestly expected exoneration and freedom from prison, but according to this passage, what was Paul's ultimate hope, and why?

7. TRUTH SEARCH

   Read the following verses, and describe what it means to "exalt Christ" on a practical basis:
   Romans 12:1

   I Corinthians 6:20

   II Corinthians 5:9

8. What does the phrase "to live is Christ, to die is gain" mean? (See the following for insight: Philippians 3:20-21; John 14:1-3; John 17:24.)

9. Read Philippians 1:22-26. Identify what is "very much better" and the reasons Paul desires to "remain on in the flesh."

Reflection

If you're like me, you sit in wonder at Paul's perspective. He would rather die and be with Christ, which makes sense when we're really fixing our hope on the things of eternity. He also recognizes that the Lord has a purpose for him while he remains in the flesh. The same is true for us. No matter how difficult our circumstances, the Lord has a purpose for us, and that is to exalt Him. We honor Him most when we recognize Him, His strength, His power, His presence in every detail of our lives, and rest in His sovereignty, obey His Word, rejoice even in the most dire of circumstances. Our response to the trials that the Lord brings our way enables us to be His witnesses in a lost and dying world of people who experience the same things we do, yet without the Lord. Psalm 31, 62, and 73 are three of my favorite places to go when I'm struggling to exalt Christ through the ups and downs of my life. Let the Lord into the corners of your heart. By faith believe His Word to be true. Thank Him for your trials knowing He will use them to teach you more about Him and His purposes in your growth and dependence.

DAY THREE

☐ Read Philippians

@ DIGGING DEEPER

As believers we've been transformed. We're new creatures in Christ. God has adopted us into the family of God, and has forgiven us all our sins and has set us free from guilt (remember, our *position in Christ* is absolutely secure because it rests on Jesus Christ). We've been given free access to the throne of grace; the Lord Jesus listens to our prayers and His Spirit empowers us to live in obedience to Him. We have His Holy Word that tells us everything we need to know about Him, His love, and His design for our lives. As children of God we have also been given hope—a hope that will never disappoint. We have the assurance of eternal life with Jesus Christ. When we walk in faith and obedience, and with an *eternal perspective*, we can find courage, steadfastness, and resolve. This perspective drove the Lord Jesus! He knew He would have to endure death on a cross, but because He knew He would return to His Father's side, He obeyed. The following passages are some of my favorites because they so clearly describe the *eternal perspective* and help me on a regular basis to be diligent and faithful to the Lord and His call in my life.

10. Read each of the passages and underline the phrases that encourage you to have an eternal perspective (for more in-depth meditation, write the passages out):

      Romans 8:16-18

      II Corinthians 4:16-18

      I Timothy 6:17-19

      Titus 2:9-14

      I Peter 1:3-9

11. Why do you think having an *eternal perspective* produces joy?

Reflection

Take at least one of these passages and apply it to your life. Consider how having an *eternal perspective* makes a difference in your life as you face trials—be they large, like a life-threatening disease, losing a job, divorce, abuse, or small, like losing your car keys, failing a test, getting lost, or being behind in your work.

DAY FOUR

☐ Read Philippians

Worthy Conduct—Philippians 1:27-30

In Philippians 1:27-30 Paul exhorts the Philippian believers to live in such a way that glorifies Jesus Christ. He encourages them as they face opposition, and reminds them that there is a price to pay when we choose to live for Him. Moreover, when we choose to live for Him the result is an abundant life—one that is full and meaningful.

"Whatever happens, conduct yourselves in a manner worthy of the gospel of Christ. Then, whether I come and see you or only hear about you in my absence, I will know that you stand firm in one spirit, contending as one man for the faith of the gospel without being frightened in any way by those who oppose you. This is a sign to them that they will be destroyed, but that you will be saved—that by God. For it has been granted to you on behalf of Christ not only to believe on Him, but also to suffer for Him, since you are going through the same struggle you saw I had, and now hear that I still have." —Philippians 1:27-30, NIV

12. Based upon this passage, for what purpose are we to conduct ourselves in a manner worthy of the gospel of Christ?

13. Why do we need to "contend as one man for the faith of the gospel"?

14. a. What two things have been granted to us on behalf of Christ?

b. Why is suffering part of being a Christian (see II Timothy 3:12, I Peter 1:6-9, and James 1:2-4 for insight)?

Reflection

"Many are the afflictions of the righteous, but the Lord delivers him out of them all."

—Psalm 34:19

Without trials and suffering we will never learn to trust the Lord. Thank Him for the people, health issues, or circumstances that are causing your stress, pain, sorrow, frustration, or anxiety. Thank Him for using these experiences to draw you closer to Him. Thank Him that He promises to deliver you from your affliction, and pray that until He does so you will rest in His sovereign control.

DAY FIVE

☐ Read Philippians

Real Life

Paul loved the Lord Jesus with every ounce of his being and he modeled and preached a life surrendered fully to Him. What mattered to the apostle was the glory of God, the furtherance of the gospel, and commitment to Jesus Christ in the face of all sorts of circumstances. As I read Philippians and the additional passages I have included in this lesson, I am struck by Paul's single-mindedness and the way Jesus permeates his life. In addition, I marvel at his *eternal perspective*. Paul really wanted to be with Jesus. He knew in his heart and his mind that being with Him would be so much better—far better than we can imagine—than being here on earth. Jesus Christ changed—transformed Paul's life, and He has done the same for you and me. Prayerfully consider the following questions:

15. The apostle used every opportunity to share the gospel. He considered every situation to have been orchestrated by the Lord, having a true and eternal purpose. How has this passage in Philippians helped you this week as you came in contact with the non-Christians in your life?

16. Paul's "earnest expectation and hope" was to exalt Christ in his body whether by life or by death. How has this challenged you personally?

17. Philippians 1:21 says, "For to me, to live is Christ, and to die is gain." Would you say you feel this same way? Why or why not?

Reflection

Pray that the Lord would give you strength and boldness to walk in obedience to His Word. Ask Him to show you what it means to exalt Christ with your life. Seek from Him a longing for greater intimacy with Christ and a greater desire to be with Him—looking forward to eternal life in His presence. Thank Him for the promises in His Word that assure us of our eternal inheritance and the coming of God's kingdom.

Copy Philippians 1:12-30 in the back of your book or in your journal.

"Do nothing from selfishness or empty conceit, but with humility of mind let each of you regard one another as more important than himself..."

Philippians 2:3

Transformed Relationships

Philippians 2:1-11

Our quick survey of the book of Acts showed us the extraordinary power of the gospel of Jesus Christ. The once hard-headed, timid, earthly-minded disciples were transformed into men who proclaimed the truth with jaw-dropping conviction. Because of the boldness of the apostles and the message of the gospel, city after city was thrown into confusion, and the apostles were thrown into prison for preaching Jesus Christ. In spite of the opposition, thousands and thousands of people were placing their faith in Jesus Christ, repenting of their sins, abandoning their old ways of life, and following Jesus Christ—in the power of the Holy Spirit. The result: the church of Jesus Christ was being formed, beginning in Jerusalem and Judea, and spreading into Galatia, Ephesus, Colossae, Philippi, and beyond—just as the Jesus instructed in Acts 1.

Each church (body of believers) possessed its own unique personality. As their "spiritual father," Paul wrote to many of them instructing them in Christ-like living. The Holy Spirit inspired Paul's writing, giving him exactly the right words to speak to each body and individual. How blessed we are to have the entire Bible at our fingertips, to have every bit of God's holy Word to guide us every day.

How blessed we are to have the entire Bible at our fingertips, to have every bit of God's holy Word to guide us every day.

The thrust of Paul's letter to the Philippians was to commend them for their partnership in the gospel, to encourage them in the face of imminent opposition, and to instruct them in their relationship with the Lord and with one another. True to form, the apostle maintains a Christ-centered and eternal perspective; we do well to learn from his godly example.

The believers in Philippi, as we're discovering, ardently followed the Lord and boldly proclaimed the gospel. Great joy filled Paul's heart upon every recollection of their participation in the gospel when he was among them, as well as their continuing witness in his absence. However, if there was an area in which the Philippians needed extra encouragement it was in the area of harmonious living (see also Philippians 4:2-3). Philippians 2:1-11 addresses the issue of unity by putting the Savior at the center, and leaves the reader no doubt as to the how's and why's behind singleness of purpose and selflessness.

As you begin today's lesson pray that you will be encouraged by the practicality of this passage. Ask the Lord to show you how to promote unity, to give you the desire to be selfless. Thank Him for His sacrifice, for His willingness to serve and obey the Father to the point of death on a cross. Praise Him for what His death means in your heart and life.

DAY ONE

☐ Read Philippians

Singleness of Purpose—Philippians 2:1-2

On the heels of his exhortation to stand "firm in one spirit, with one mind striving together for the faith of the gospel" in the face of opposition, Paul states the importance of singleness of mind and purpose in our relationships with each other as believers.

I like Phillip's translation of Philippians 2:1-2:

"Now if your experience of Christ's encouragement and love means anything to you, if you have known something of the fellowship of his Spirit, and all that it means in kindness and deep sympathy, do make my best hopes for you come true! Live together in harmony, live together in love, as though you had only one mind and one spirit between you."

1. Record two or three specific ways you've experienced Christ's encouragement (as described in Philippians 2:1) this week.

2. How does the reality of the Lord's encouragement, love, fellowship, kindness and sympathy in your own life contribute to harmony and single-minded relationships (see Romans 12:15, II Corinthians 13:14, Ephesians 5:2, Hebrews 4:13)?

3. Be "of the <u>same mind</u>, maintaining the <u>same love</u>, united in spirit, intent on <u>one purpose</u>" (Philippians 2:2 NASB).

    a. Whose mind do we have, according to John 15:15 and I Corinthians 2:16?

    b. What kind of love are we called to maintain? Refer back to John 13:34-35 and I John 4:7,10-11.

    c. Around whom must we unite?

Reflection

So often the Lord uses us in each others' lives to express His encouragement, love, and compassion. When we're unified around the person and work of Jesus Christ we ultimately display His glory through our love and commitment to one another. And, by the way, this passage is a picture of what Paul prays for in Philippians 1:9-11.

DAY TWO

☐ Read Philippians

Setting the Standard—Philippians 2:3-5

"The last word of this section is the keynote—"others." This was the overpowering, dominating note in the life of our Lord on earth, and because of this He died. "He came not to be ministered unto, but to minister, and to give his life a ransom for '—*others*! He lived for *others;* He died for *others*. Selfishness He knew not. Unselfish devotion for the good of *others* summed up His whole life, and in all subjection to the Father's will. For God, the Father Himself, lives, reverently be it said, for *others*. He finds His delight, His joy, in lavishing blessing on *others*. He gave His Son for *others*."[1]

4. Record Philippians 2:3-4 and underline each of the ways we demonstrate the mind of Christ, the love of Christ, and the unity of the spirit.

5. Describe what it would look like to do NOTHING from: "selfishness: self-centeredness, greediness, egocentricity; or empty conceit: an overblown sense of one's positive attributes," pride, self-love, self-worship, self-importance."[2]

6. TRUTH SEARCH

    a. Why is "humility of mind" necessary? I Peter 5:5-6.

b. What does it look like, according to Romans 12:10?

7. Read Philippians 2:4. Why do we need this reminder?

8. According to Philippians 2:5, whose attitude are we to emulate and why?

Reflection

As you close your Bible today, consider the impact of these three verses on your life. How will you apply them to your life and in your relationships? Pray and ask the Lord for the desire and willingness to walk humbly before Him and the people He places in your life.

DAY THREE

☐ Read Philippians

⊚ DIGGING DEEPER

Is it possible to do nothing from selfishness or empty conceit, to walk in humility, regarding others as more important than ourselves, with the same attitude that Jesus had? No, in the flesh it is impossible. But, remember, we are transformed, new creatures in Christ! We are indwelt with the Holy Spirit of God and His power. Today's lesson focuses on both our position in Christ—who we are because of what Christ did on our behalf—and our sanctification—the daily process of becoming like Christ in our attitudes and actions. Pray for wisdom as you begin!

9. a. Romans 6:4 says: "Therefore, we have been buried with Him through baptism unto death, in order that as Christ was raised from the dead through the glory of the Father, so <u>we too might walk in newness of life</u>." What is the result of our being baptized into the death of Christ (keep your eyes on the text)?

　　b. Romans 6:5 –7,11 says: "For if we have become united with Him in the likeness of His death, certainly we shall be also in the likeness of His resurrection, knowing this, that our old self was crucified with Him, that our body of sin might be done away with, that we should no longer be slaves to sin; for he who has died is freed from sin….Even so, consider yourselves to be dead to sin, but alive to God in Christ Jesus."

　　　• What happened to our "old self" and our "body of sin" (keep your eyes on the text)?

　　　• Underline each of the phrases which describe your position in Christ.

- What is our relationship to sin (keep your eyes on the text)?

c. Romans 6:12-13 says: "Therefore do not let sin reign in your mortal body that you should obey its lusts, and do not go on presenting the members of your body to sin as instruments of unrighteousness; but present yourselves to God as those alive from the dead, and your members as instruments of righteousness to God."

- What are we instructed to do "as those alive from the dead" (keep your eyes on the text)?

10. a. Colossians 3:1-4 says: "If then you have been raised up with Christ, keep seeking the things above, where Christ is, seated at the right hand of God. Set your mind on the things above, not on the things that are on earth. For you have died and your life is hidden with Christ in God. When Christ, who is our life, is revealed, then you also will be revealed with Him in glory."

- What is our position in Christ according to this passage (keep your eyes on the text)?

- What are we instructed to do in order to remind ourselves of our standing in Christ (keep your eyes on the text)?

b. Colossians 3:5-11 says: "Therefore consider the members of your earthly body as dead to immorality, impurity, passion, evil desire and greed, which amounts to idolatry. For it is on account of these things that the wrath of God will come, and in them you also once walked, when you were living in them. But now you also, put them all aside: anger, wrath, malice, slander, and abusive speech from your mouth. Do not lie to one another, since you laid aside the old self with its evil practices, and have put on the new self who is being renewed to a true knowledge according to the image of the One who created him...."

- What must you do with the "old self?" With the "new self?"

We have been crucified with Christ. Our old self (with all of its passions and desires) has been put to death, nailed to the cross. We have been raised up with Christ—dead to sin and alive to God. Every day we can make the choice to live in light of our position in Christ by choosing to believe that what Bible says about us is true.

11. TRUTH SEARCH:

a. According to the following texts, what is the source of power for our new life in Christ? See Romans 8:6, 13, Galatians 5:16, Ephesians 3:16, 20-21, Colossians 3:16.

b. With these passages in mind, how is the attitude in Philippians 2:3-5 possible?

Reflection

We need to be saturating our minds with the Word—determined to lay aside the old self and to put on the new. We must rely on the power of His Spirit to enable us to walk in newness of life. Praise Him for freeing you from sin—its penalty and its power. Thank Him for teaching you how to walk in newness of life.

DAY FOUR

☐ Read Philippians

Christ our example—Philippians 2:6-11

Jesus Christ is the centerpiece of Christianity and is marvelously described in Philippians 2:6-11. Jesus Christ emptied Himself not of His divine nature or attributes, but of the outward and visible manifestation of deity. He did not cease to be God but voluntarily took the place of subjection to God. Jesus became like a man, chose to be guided by the Holy Spirit and to receive instruction from His Father. In all things the Lord Jesus Christ became like us. Hebrews 2:17 says, "Therefore, He had to be made like His brethren in all things, that He might become a merciful and faithful high priest in things pertaining to God, to make propitiation [to satisfy God's wrath] for the sins of the people." This is staggering truth. May we never cease to be amazed and grateful.

12. a. List the different ways Jesus demonstrated humility according to Philippians 2:6-8.

b. Where did the Lord's obedience take Him and why?

13. Read Philippians 2:9-11. What was the reward for Christ's humble obedience?

14. TRUTH SEARCH:

Read the following and record what you learn about Christ's exaltation: Matthew 28:18, Ephesians 1:20-23, Hebrews 1:1-3.

Reflection

"One day every knee will bow in heaven, and on earth, and under the earth"—whether saved or unsaved—and will acknowledge that Jesus Christ is Lord—all to the glory of the Father. What a great day that will be! Thank Him for His willingness to go to the cross on your behalf. Thank Him for forgiving you. Acknowledge today that Jesus Christ is Lord of your life.

DAY FIVE

☐ Read Philippians

Real Life

Philippians 2:5-11 reminds us of the significance of Christ's voluntary choice to go to the cross—the most humiliating form of death—for you and for me. The words also emphasize that all authority has been given to Him—in heaven and on earth. He is in charge and in control. Such security there is in knowing Him. On a more pragmatic level, Jesus Christ has called us to follow His example in our relationships with one another, and has given us everything we need to walk in obedience. He knows we cannot do so without His power.

15. How are you contributing to the unity of the body of Christ; in other words, how will you apply Philippians 2:1-5 in your relationships at church and Bible study, in your marriage, your friendships, and your job relationships?

16. Name one specific area where you recognize the need to consider someone else as more important than yourself.

17. Commit Philippians 2:1-5 to memory. Allow the Spirit of God to use the Word of God to help you obey the will of God.

Reflection

We cannot possibly imitate Jesus Christ without the power of the Holy Spirit. Ephesians 5:18 reminds us, "…do not get drunk with wine, for that is dissipation, but be filled with the Spirit…." Being filled with the Spirit is a moment by moment choice that we make to allow Him to control our thoughts, emotions, choices, actions, and will. It means that we must submit ourselves to the Lordship of Christ, and *practice the presence of God* throughout our day. As we do so, He will give us the power we need to follow Jesus Christ's example and to consider others as more important than ourselves.

Copy Philippians 2:1-11 in the back of your book or in your journal.

1 Ironside, pg. 37
2 McCutcheon, pg. 124, 205, 505

"Do all things without grumbling or disputing; that you may prove yourselves to be blameless and innocent, children of God above reproach in the midst of a crooked and perverse generation."

Philippians 2:14-15

Transformed Living

Philippians 2:12-30

Though my husband and I have lived in our suburban neighborhood for five years, we have not yet been able to have a real conversation about Jesus Christ with even one of our neighbors. It's not that we don't want to—we do! But their busy lives, lack of interest, or perhaps fear keep them from getting too close. I pray often for each of our neighbors and their children, that they will come to know Jesus Christ as their Lord and Savior, and that Bob and I will be ready when the time comes to proclaim the truth. Until then, this passage in Philippians reminds me how essential it is that my daily life shines brightly for Jesus Christ.

We are called to be Christ's ambassadors.

The message of the gospel is one of repentance, love, and forgiveness, centered on the person and work of the Lord Jesus Christ. In fact, Paul reminds us in this passage that we appear as lights in the midst of a crooked and perverse generation—we are called to be Christ's ambassadors. Don't forget, however, that the backdrop of this call is the humility and exaltation of Jesus Christ our Lord (Philippians 2:6-11). We must occupy ourselves with Him, striving to honor and glorify Him in both word and deed—following His example in His power. Pray as you begin that the Lord will use His Word to compel you to let your light shine brightly for His glory.

DAY ONE

☐ Read Philippians

Walking in Obedience—Philippians 2:12-16

When you placed your faith in Jesus Christ you were immediately delivered from the **penalty** of sin. Ephesians 2:8-9 says, "For by grace you have been saved through faith, and that not of yourselves, it is the gift of God, not as a result of works that no one should boast." As children of God we know that in eternity we will be delivered from the **presence** of sin. On a day to day basis we are being delivered from the **power** of sin. It is this daily deliverance that Paul is talking about in Philippians 2:12-13. As you study this passage keep on the forefront of your mind the security of your <u>position in Christ</u>.

1. Read Philippians 2:12. For what does Paul commend the Philippians?

As you read Philippians 2:12 take note that the exhortation is to "work out" your salvation, not to "work for" your salvation! <u>The New Testament in Modern English</u> paraphrases Philippians 2:12-13, "be keener than ever to work out the salvation that God has given you with a proper sense of awe and responsibility. For it is God who is at work within you, giving you the will and the power to achieve his purpose."

2. What does it look like on a daily basis to "work out your salvation with fear and trembling"?

3. TRUTH SEARCH:

Study the following passages, and based upon God's Word, how do you know that this phrase is not inferring that your eternal salvation is uncertain? Use Scripture to support your answer.

John 10:27-29

Hebrews 13:15

I John 5:11-13

4. Look ahead to Philippians 2:14-16 and record what it looks like to live in obedience to God and His Word. Keep your eyes on the text.

5. Why are we told to "work out our salvation with **fear and trembling**," or "with a proper sense of awe and responsibility"?

6. Compare Philippians 2:13 with Philippians 1:6. What does it mean to you personally to know that "God is at work in you, giving you the will and the power to achieve His purpose"?

7. TRUTH SEARCH

a. What insight do you gain from the following verses regarding the Lord's involvement in obedient living? John 15:4-5; Galatians 2:20; Philippians 4:13.

b. Review the following verses and record the part we play in obedient living?

Romans 6:12-13

Galatians 5:16-25

Colossians 3:5-10

Reflection

Elisabeth Elliot once said, "Struggling is just another word for postponed obedience." Are you "struggling" to obey the Lord in a certain area of your life? Talk to the Lord about it—tell Him everything. Thank Him for forgiving you at the cross of Calvary. Thank Him for His unconditional love. Then review the promises found in this lesson and claim them to be true in your specific situation. Ask the Lord to give you the power to make godly choices, and trust Him to give you the ability to conquer your sin. Remember, "we follow a Conqueror."

DAY TWO

☐ Read Philippians

Living As Lights in the World—Philippians 2:14-18

It is so important for us to remember Who we serve and represent. In addition, we can take great comfort in knowing that the Christian life is impossible to live apart from the Word of God and the power of His Spirit working in and through our lives. Let me encourage you to become men and women of the Word spending time daily at the feet of the Savior. How you spend your time and how you live your life make a difference in the midst of a crooked and perverse generation.

8.   Look specifically at Philippians 2:14-16. For what purpose are we to "do all things without grumbling and disputing"?

9.   a. Philippians 2:14-15 says: "Do all things without grumbling or disputing, that you may prove yourselves to be blameless and innocent, children of God above reproach in the midst of a crooked and perverse generation, among whom you appear as lights in the world" (NASB). Define the following words:

Blameless:

Innocent:

God's child:

Above reproach:

b. Why do these four characteristics set us apart from the world?

"Christ is the light of the world, and real Christians are lights in the world. When God raises up a good man in any place, He sets up a light there. Christians must shine as well as be sincere. The doctrine and example of consistent believers will tend to enlighten others, and to direct their way to Christ and holiness, even as the light-house warns mariners to avoid rocks, and directs their course into the harbor."[1]

10. Recount a time in your life when someone took notice of your Christian behavior and commented upon it. How did it make you feel?

11. Look carefully at Philippians 2:14-16. Why is it important that we "hold fast" the word of life?

12. Paul's heart for the children of God is evident throughout this letter. What in particular brings Paul joy according to Philippians 2:16-18?

Reflection

Ask the Lord to give you wisdom and sensitivity as you interact with the world around you. Ask Him to help you "do all things without grumbling or disputing" and to remind you that you are a light in the world…shine brightly for Him!

DAY THREE

☐ Read Philippians

@ DIGGING DEEPER

Paul continues on a more personal level by introducing us to two people, Timothy and Epaphroditus. Paul loves these two men and values their friendship and their hard work in the ministry. I concur! There is nothing more important and more meaningful than partnering with the people of God. As you read you will learn much about Paul's relationship with these men, and you will find their examples well worth imitating. Before we look at the passage in Philippians, let's consider the value of having and being a kindred spirit by examining Paul and Timothy's relationship.

In Philippians 2:20 Paul refers to Timothy as his one and only "kindred spirit." "Similar", "matching", "parallel", "allied" are all words that describe a kindred spirit. Paul and Timothy's relationship illustrates for us a true picture of like-minded love and service.

13. Look at the following passages and ask yourself these questions:

a. What can I learn from Paul and Timothy's relationship?

b. What can I learn from Paul and Timothy's heart for the Lord and His ministry?

c. What qualities make up a kindred spirit?

Acts 16:1-5 (notice Paul met Timothy a short time before they arrived in Philippi)

I Timothy 1:1-3

I Timothy 1:13-20

I Timothy 4:6-16

I Timothy 5:23

I Timothy 6:11-16, 20-21

II Timothy 1:2-7

II Timothy 3:14-17

II Timothy 4:9-16 (notice where some of Paul's friends ended up)

d. How can I apply this to my life today?

Reflection

Pray and ask the Lord to develop the qualities of a kindred spirit in your own heart and life. Pray that He will bless you with the kind of friendship Paul and Timothy shared.

DAY FOUR

☐ Read Philippians

Kindred Spirits Illustrated—Philippians 2:19-30

This last passage of Philippians 2 gives us a picture of all that Paul has been addressing so far in this epistle. Through the lives and ministries of Timothy and Epaphroditus we see Christ-like love, selfless service, and unwavering commitment to the gospel.

14. Read Philippians 2:19-24. For what purpose did Paul want to send Timothy to Philippi?

15. Look carefully at this passage and record all of Paul's reasons for trusting Timothy to carry out his wishes.

16. a. With these verses in mind, record any additional insight you gain into the description of a "kindred spirit."

b. What will it take for you to be this kind of a friend?

17. Though we do not have a great deal of information about Epaphroditus, what we do have is instructive. Look closely at Philippians 2:26-30. What do you learn about his heart for the Philippian church, and about him as a man of God?

18. According to Philippians 2:27, how did Paul know that Epaphroditus' visit would give the Philippians great joy?

Reflection

In a few weeks a dear friend of mine turns 50. In celebration of this great milestone, I have compiled a memory book filled with notes from many women who have been influenced by my friend throughout her life. As I paste the notes addressed to this godly woman into the book, I feel like I'm reading over the shoulders of many women who, like Timothy and Epaphroditus, serve the Lord with great dedication—largely because of my friend's Paul-like influence in their lives. I know she considers many of them "kindred spirits." Is there someone who took you under his/her wing and taught you how to follow Jesus? Write and thank him/her for teaching you to follow the Lord, to love His Word, and to serve Him passionately. Pray about becoming a "Paul" in someone's life yourself!

DAY FIVE

☐ Read Philippians

Real Life

19. a. What tends to "trip you up" and cause you to fall short of the life to which God has called you?

b. What have you learned from this passage that will help you live in obedience?

20. Who is there in your life that loves you and encourages you like Paul, Timothy, and Epaphroditus? In other words, who is your kindred spirit and why?

21. How will you apply what you have learned from this passage in your life this week?

Reflection

It is my prayer that this passage of Philippians will challenge you afresh in your walk with the Lord. He wants nothing more than hearts given over fully to Him. I am convinced that the more we deepen our understanding of our salvation, the more we will strive to live in obedience to His Word. In a recent conversation someone told me how desperately she desired to keep her walk with the Lord vibrant. It scared her to think how easy it would be to step onto the path of mediocrity. I encouraged her with the verses we've studied this week: "work out your salvation with fear and trembling; for it is God who is at work in you, both to will and to work for His good pleasure." We need a healthy sense of fear and reverence toward God. He is holy and righteous! Only because of Him can we boast of forgiveness of sin, a hope that will not disappoint, and the promise of eternal life. Yet, at the same time we rest in His loving arms and His mighty power that allows us to shine brightly in our sin-scarred world. If you are on the edge of the path of mediocrity, reach out to the Lord. Ask Him to revitalize your heart, to bring to mind all that He has done for you. Go back and meditate upon Philippians 2:6-11. Praise and worship the One to whom all authority has been given, and rejoice in the fact that He is your Savior.

Copy Philippians 2:12-30 in the back of your book or in your journal.

1 Henry, Scott, pg. 239

"More than that, I count all things to be loss in view of the surpassing value of knowing Christ Jesus my Lord, for whom I have suffered the loss of all things, and count them but rubbish in order that I may gain Christ."

Philippians 3:8

Transformed Heart

Philippians 3:1-11

Over twenty- years ago, I sat in a room filled with several hundred men and women who were being trained to serve Jesus Christ on university campuses both at home and abroad. I found myself particularly challenged by a speaker who, quoting from the book of Philippians, challenged us to "count all things as loss in view of the surpassing value of knowing Christ Jesus our Lord." He exhorted us to live in light of eternity, to surrender everything to the Lord—dreams, desires, and plans—and follow Him. With great fervency I made a commitment to live for Christ and penned my heart-felt desire in the front of my brand-new Bible. My relationship with the Savior was new and fresh, and I wanted to be passionate about living for Him and sharing the Gospel. Philippians chapter three became then and remains one of my most favorite passages in the Bible. I loved the strength of Paul's words and the depth of his conviction. I wanted to be just like him in my devotion and service to the Lord.

Passionate living is a matter of the heart.

People's faces, specific places, significant moments following that day of commitment wrap themselves around the memories of my soul and remind me of the many of the lessons the Lord has taught me; mainly, that passionate living is a matter of the heart. As I have continued studying Philippians, I have noticed with more and more clarity that Paul counted everything as loss in view of the surpassing value of *knowing* Christ Jesus his Lord. Paul's life was centered around knowing the Savior personally and intimately; his mission: making Him known.

It is my prayer that your study of this chapter of Philippians will motivate you in your relationship with the Lord. Ask Him to use this passage to reveal those things in your life that might keep you from living passionately, and surrender your heart and will to the Lord today.

DAY ONE

☐ Read Philippians

The True Believer—Philippians 3:1-7

The apostle begins the conclusion of his letter, but is sidetracked by the Holy Spirit, who leads him to remind the Philippians, and all believers, to "beware of the dogs, beware of the evil workers, beware of the false circumcision." Philippians 3:2. Throughout the history of the church there have always been false teachers seeking to steal our liberty in Christ, robbing us of our joy, and turning the grace of God into either licentiousness or legalism. Paul warns by reminding us to rejoice in the Lord—joy in the Lord is a "safeguard." If we're rejoicing in Christ, our eyes are on Him and not on our circumstances or our feelings, and our hearts will be filled with Him and with what is true.

1. a. Why is joy in the Lord a "safeguard" for us?

    b. Why would the exhortation to "rejoice" be worthy of repeating?

2. How is Paul's warning in Philippians 3:2 applicable to us today?

3.   a. Describe the "true circumcision" (true believer) as recorded in Philippians 3:3.

    b. Look at Romans 2:28-29. What sets the true believer apart from the "religious" and "false" believer?

4.   a. Look carefully at Philippians 3:4-6. Before knowing Christ Jesus as his Savior, where did Paul put his confidence, and why?

    b. According to Philippians 3:7, how did Paul feel about his accomplishments after becoming a believer? Why?

5.   In what areas of life are you tempted to put your confidence, and why?

6. Why does the "true believer" not have to put his/her confidence in the flesh?

Reflection

The longer I walk with the Lord the more freedom I experience! I am so thankful that the Lord wants me to find my confidence in Him, not in my accomplishments or abilities. He desires and deserves the glory for whatever good comes of our lives; He is the source of our strength, our abilities, and our very lives. Pray that you will learn to find your confidence in Him and experience freedom from the pressure of performance. Pray you will learn in an even deeper way that His love for you is absolutely not dependent upon your successes or failures, but upon the death, burial, and resurrection of Jesus Christ.

DAY TWO

☐ Read Philippians

The Surpassing Value Of Knowing Christ—Philippians 3:7-8

From a Jewish standpoint Paul had it all! Notice how he makes it clear that he had reason to be confident in the flesh—more than most. He was from the right family, went to all the right schools, graduated top in his class after studying under the greatest teacher of the law (or so he thought at the time). Paul even claimed to be blameless! Then he met Jesus Christ. Our worldly accomplishments pale in comparison to the glory of the Lord Jesus.

7.   a. Write out Philippians 3:7-8.

   b. Underline the words that describe Paul's feelings about his human achievements after meeting Christ.

8.   What value does he place on knowing Christ? Keep your eyes on the text.

9.   a. What value do you place on knowing Christ? Consider the things in your life that draw you toward Him. Is knowing Him a priority in your day? Are you drawn to His Word? What is your heart's deepest desire?

b. What things tempt you away from knowing Him: your career path, your money, your children, athletics, school work, a relationship, your pleasures?

10. Why is knowing Him so important for us as believers?

Reflection

When I read Philippians 3:8 for the first time, Paul's passion for knowing the Lord both convicted and encouraged me to question how deeply I valued my relationship with Him. It never ceases to amaze me that the great and mighty God wants us to know Him, and not simply intellectually, but intimately. The better we know the Lord, the more fervently we will love and obey Him.

> ᘓ STUDY TOOLS: COPYING SCRIPTURE
>
> I urge you to read Philippians everyday and to copy each passage studied in the back of your study book or in your personal journal. You will be reminded to do both throughout the study. In my personal experience, when I copy a book of Scripture, I gain so much more as I familiarize myself with the book. Philippians has only four chapters and should not take long to copy, and the time it does take is well worth the effort.

DAY THREE

© Digging Deeper

☐ Read Philippians

One of the many things we can learn from Paul's relationship with the Lord is the fact that being a Christian is not meant to be a religion—a system of do's and don'ts—but is meant to be a relationship—deepening, vital, and growing. The Lord, as we see over and over in His Word, desires for us to relate to Him on a very personal level. He calls us to intimacy by showing through the Psalms and through the many prayers of the Bible, that we can pour out our hearts to Him. We can be open, honest, and truly ourselves before Him. His love never wanes, and is unconditional. Our relationship with Him, above any other relationship we'll ever have, is absolutely secure. He has demonstrated His love for and commitment to us through His Son. Why wouldn't we want to know Him?

11. Look up the following verses and record some of the benefits of knowing the Lord.

    Psalm 9:10

    Psalm 62:8

    Psalm 147:5

    Ephesians 1:17-21

12. What are some of the things He wants us to know about Him? Job 19:25; Psalm 56:8-9; Jeremiah 9:24-25; Ephesians 3:16-21.

13. With what kind of attitude should we approach knowing the Lord? I Chronicles 28:9; Hosea 6:3; Philippians 3:8.

Reflection

As you read the Word keep track of all the passages that remind you of the benefits of knowing the Lord. Record the different things He wants you to know about Him. Praise Him for making Himself known to you through His Son.

DAY FOUR

☐ Read Philippians

Righteousness in Christ—Philippians 3:9-11

This week's lesson is focused on our relationship with the Lord—knowing Him intimately. I often marvel that He wants us to know Him, to seek Him, to talk with Him! As I take time to meditate on those truths I also stand in awe of the fact that it is Jesus Christ's shed blood on the cross that makes it possible for a sinner like me to enter into relationship with Him. Today's lesson looks at what it means to be made righteous *in Christ*—a foundational truth of the Christian life. Pray that the Lord will give you the ability to comprehend this great truth.

14. How does Paul hope to be found in Christ, according to Philippians 3:9?

15. a. Read Romans 3:23-26; 4:1-5 and describe the only way to obtain righteousness. Keep in mind that "justified" means to be "declared righteous."

    b. How does "our own" righteousness differ from the righteousness of Christ (see Romans 3:10-18 for insight)?

c. What do you learn about your righteousness from these passages?

16. TRUTH SEARCH:

Compare the following with Philippians 3:10 and record what you learn about the things Paul wanted to know about the Lord.

a. The power of His resurrection: Romans 6:8-10; Romans 8:1,38 and 39; II Corinthians 5:17; Colossians 2:10 and 3:10.

b. The fellowship of His sufferings: II Corinthians 1:3-5; Hebrews 12:2-3; I Peter 2:21-23.

c. Being conformed to His death: Romans 6:6-7; Galatians 2:20; Colossians 3:3-5.

Reflection

The more you and I learn about the gift God has given us, the more we will "count all things as loss in view of the surpassing value of knowing Christ Jesus our Lord." Sinful, selfish, enemies of God, helpless, prideful, and hopeless are just a few of the dark words that describe where we stood before coming to know Jesus Christ. Sin separated us from God, and God demanded payment for sin. In His immeasurable love, God reached out to us through His Son. "For God so loved the world [you and me and everyone else] that He gave His only begotten Son, that whoever believes in Him will not perish, but will have everlasting life" (John 3:16). The moment we placed our faith in Christ we became righteous in God's eyes, because He sees us through the shed blood of His Son. "Therefore having been justified [declared righteous] by faith, we have peace with God through our Lord Jesus Christ, through whom also we have obtained our introduction by faith into this grace in which we stand; and we exult in hope of the glory of God" (Romans 5:1-2). Stop right here and thank God for saving you and clothing you in the righteousness of Christ.

DAY FIVE

☐ Read Philippians

Real Life

17. How can knowing the Lord, the power of His resurrection, and the fellowship of His sufferings, and being conformed to His death actually make a difference in your life on a practical level?

18. What steps are you taking to deepen your understanding of these truths?

Reflection

Is there anything in your life that you are hanging onto, anything that you count as more valuable than knowing Christ? Is there anything that keeps you from living passionately for Christ; in other words, are you willing to open your hand and give Him your greatest treasure and dream? Why or why not? Talk with the Lord about it and ask Him to free you from whatever is holding you back from "counting all things as loss" in comparison to knowing and walking with Him.

Copy Philippians 3:1-11 in the back of your book or in your journal.

"I press on toward the goal
of the upward call of God in
Christ Jesus."

Philippians 3:14

Transformed Goal

Philippians 3:12-4:1

Just the other day I was talking with a young woman who is standing at a crossroads in her life. One road promises to satisfy her flesh—instant gratification but short-lived—and requires compromise in her walk with the Lord. The other road requires that she surrender everything she holds dear, and take up her cross and follow Jesus Christ—the rewards will be rich both in this life and the one to come—but they will take a lifetime to acquire. Which road will she choose? Which road have you chosen?

Which road will she choose?
Which road have you chosen?

Living passionately for Christ is an attitude of the heart, an attitude that says: "I count all things as loss in view of the surpassing value of knowing Christ Jesus as Lord." Paul's desire was to "know Him, the power of His resurrection, the fellowship of His sufferings, being conformed to His death," and his growing knowledge of the Savior and his deepening devotion gave him great purpose and hope. In Philippians 3:12-4:1, Paul's fervent pursuit of the goal—"the upward call of God in Christ Jesus,"—reveals his passion for Christ. Remember the earmark of his zeal was to know Christ Jesus, and the effort was aimed toward eternity. He had the "day of Christ" in mind in both chapters one and two. He desired to die and be with Christ—considering that to be "very much better" than anything else. The whole of Philippians points us to Jesus Christ and the hope that is ours in heaven.

As you begin your study of this passage ask the Lord to open the eyes of your heart, to create in you a willingness to take up your cross and follow Christ—passionately.

DAY ONE

☐ Read Philippians

The Goal—Philippians 3:12-16

Someone once said, "If you aim at nothing you'll hit it every time." It's hard to live passionately without having a goal. Conversely, it's hard to live passionately if we have too many things we're trying to accomplish. Philippians 3:12-16 teaches us to aim at one thing—the upward call of God in Christ Jesus. Our pursuit needs to be a purposeful, conscious decision to practice His presence in every realm of life. Prayerfully begin your study today, asking the Lord to help you aim for the highest goal—His eternal glory.

1. Look closely at Philippians 3:12-14. What action verbs describe the effort Paul put into   knowing Christ?

2. Paul's great desire was to be like Christ—to be found in His righteousness, and ultimately to be with Christ in eternity. According to Philippians 3:13-14, what were the things Paul did in his effort to lay hold of Christ Jesus?

3. a. Based upon all that we've studied in Philippians, why is it essential that we "forget what lies behind"?

b. Are there particular events, people, choices, or sins from your past that you need to forget? If so, lay those memories at the foot of the cross. Thank the Lord Jesus for declaring you righteous!

c. What is it that lies ahead?

4. a. Compare Philippians 3:14 with I Timothy 6:12-19. What is the goal of the believer?

b. What does it look like practically to "press on" toward this objective?

5. a. Philippians 3:15 says, "Let us therefore, as many as are perfect [that is, "mature"], have this attitude; and if in anything you have a different attitude, God will reveal that also to you." How is one to mature/grow in Christ (for insight look at Philippians 3:7-15)?

b. What attitude will result?

6.   Read Philippians 3:16 in context with our passage of study. By what standard are we to keep living and why?

Reflection

Paul describes for us his purpose and focal point—Jesus Christ. Press on, lay hold, reach forward, strive for the goal of the upward call of God in Christ Jesus. This section is replete with verbs that describe the effort Paul put into knowing Christ. His goal was to be with Christ in eternity and to live for Christ on earth. Living passionately for Jesus involves pursuing Him with fervency and conducting ourselves in such a way that reflects His holy standard.

Pray that He will give you the desire to live passionately for Him both in your devotional time and your daily life.

DAY TWO

☐ Read Philippians

Enemies of the Cross—Philippians 3:17-19

Philippians chapter three begins with a warning: "beware of the dogs, beware of the evil workers, beware of the false circumcision." False teachers were abundant in Paul's day and continue to abound in ours—teachers who discredit the cross of Jesus Christ, who minimize and even mock the work Jesus Christ did on our behalf. Paul exhorts the Philippians to follow his example and the example of others who live for Jesus.

7.   a. Read Philippians 3:18-19. Describe the enemies of the cross.

        b. What will be the end result of those who are enemies of the cross?

8.   TRUTH SEARCH:

    Look up the following passages and record what you learn about the enemies of the cross: II Peter 2:1-3; I John 2:18-22; Jude 16-19.

9. There were enemies of the cross in Paul's day, just as there are in ours. Describe a time in your life when you encountered an enemy of the cross.

Reflection

Keep in mind that these three verses fall in the context of Philippians chapter three, a chapter which lifts us to the heights of devotion to Christ and reminds us of the worthlessness of our own confidence and earthly gain. Chapter 3 reminds us of our position in Christ and of the hope that is ours because of all He has done for us. Worship the Lord Jesus for submitting Himself to the Father and subjecting Himself to the cross. Praise Him for initiating a relationship with you. Thank Him for no longer calling you His enemy but instead, His child.

DAY THREE

☐ Read Philippians

@ Digging Deeper

Life in this technological world is a fast-paced, non-stop whirlwind of activity. We barely have the time to sleep between events, let alone to think about the things of eternity. Jesus repeatedly reminds us of the importance of living for Him now, being ready for His return and prepared for life in eternity. Luke 12:35-40 is one of my favorite passages because it reminds me—with a certain urgency—that Jesus is coming back, and that I need to be ready.

10. Read Luke 12:35-40.

11. Who are the different people involved in this story and for whom are they waiting?

12. What does it mean to be "dressed in readiness"?

13. Compare this passage with I Thessalonians 5:1-11. What is going to happen on the day of the Lord's return?

14. How are we instructed to prepare ourselves?

15. Are you ready? Why or why not?

Reflection

Maybe you are at a crossroads in your life—faced with the decision to follow Christ even if it means giving up the things you hold dear to your heart. What is holding you back from laying your life down for Christ? What have you learned from this passage, and Philippians 3, that will help you live in light of eternity?

DAY FOUR

☐ Read Philippians

Our True Citizenship—Philippians 3:20-4:1

My husband always reminds me that I'm a "citizen of heaven on loan from God." I find his reminder very helpful as I strive to live for Christ in and admidst the world's distractions, and this passage is especially encouraging as it takes our position in Christ all the way to heaven; it's a motivating section of Philippians. Pray that the Lord will use this passage in your life to give you hope and joy as you await His return.

16. According to Philippians 3:20, we are citizens of heaven eagerly awaiting the return of our Savior. Based upon what you've learned so far, why are we eagerly waiting for Jesus?

17. a. Look specifically at Philippians 3:21. When Christ does appear, what will happen to us?

    b. What further insight do you gain from II Corinthians 15:50-53; II Thessalonians 4:13-17.

    c. According to I Peter 1:13-16 and I John 3:2-3, how can knowing this affect our lives right now?

18. a. Read Philippians 4:1. What is Paul's exhortation in this verse?

    b. As you look back at chapter three, upon whom are we to stand firm, and why? Use Scripture to support your answer.

19. Are you eager for Jesus to return? Why or why not?

Reflection

Dr. Bill Bright, the founder and president of Campus Crusade for Christ, recently went home to be with the Lord. The "upward call of God in Christ Jesus" was Dr. Bright's goal, and his example has compelled countless others to follow in his steps. Dr. Bright lived his life anticipating the Lord's return and longing to be in His presence. As a result, his great love for Jesus Christ, his obedience to God's call, and his commitment to the proclamation of the gospel profoundly influenced the entire world. Pray that you will keep the Lord's return and the reality of eternity with Him fresh on your heart. Make a commitment to share the gospel with someone this week—anticipating His return!

DAY FIVE

☐ Read Philippians

Real Life

Remember that living passionately for Christ begins with having Jesus at the center of our hearts. The better we understand what the gospel means in our own lives, the better we will understand <u>how</u> to live for Him and the more we will <u>want</u> to live for Him. Praise the Lord for calling you His child, for giving you eternal citizenship, for transforming your life and promising to transform your body upon His return. Praise Him for His love and His Son. Ask Him to help these truths penetrate your being.

20. How can we apply Philippians 3:12-16 to our lives in a practical way? In other words, what does it look like to press on, lay hold, and reach forward in our personal lives?

21. Think of one way that you can remind yourself of your heavenly citizenship this week.

Reflection

Finish your time in the word by reading Revelation 22:1-5 aloud and enjoy a glimpse of heaven, and as you do picture yourself there in the presence of your Savior.

"And he showed me a river of the water of life, clear as crystal, coming from the throne of God and of the Lamb, in the middle of its street. And on either side of the river was the tree of life, bearing twelve kinds of fruit, yielding its fruit every month; and the leaves of the tree were for the healing of the nations .And there shall no longer by any curse; and the throne of God and of the Lamb shall be in it, and His bond-servants shall serve Him; and they shall see His face, and His name shall be on their foreheads. And there shall no longer be any night; and they shall not have need of the light of a lamp nor the light of the sun, because the Lord God shall illumine them; and they shall reign forever and ever."—Revelation 22:1-5

Copy Philippians 3:12-4:1 in the back of your book or in your journal.

Finally bretheren, whatever is true, whatever is honorable, whatever is right, whatever is pure, whatever is lovely, whatever is of good repute, if there is any excellence, and anything worthy of praise, let your mind dwell on these things."

Philippians 4:8

Transformed Mind

A Heavenly Mindset—Philippians 4:2-9

While serving on the staff of Campus Crusade for Christ, I had the privilege of meeting a man named Bud Hinkson. At the time Bud served as a director for Campus Crusade for Christ in what was then the Eastern Bloc of Europe—countries living under communist control. Never before had I met a man so filled with joy and passion for the Lord Jesus Christ. His smile spread across his face as he talked about people coming to Christ in the countries behind the "Iron Curtain." Bud talked about sitting with young believers in the East Bloc and teaching through passages of Scripture that seemed to roll off his tongue with no effort at all!

In 1986 several hundred Campus Crusade for Christ staff and students spent the summer in most of the Eastern Bloc countries. My husband and I led a group of 70 Campus Crusade staff and students into Poland. Broken down into several teams and spread across the Baltic Coast, we spent our time telling vacationing Poles the good news of Jesus Christ. At the end of our project all the teams gathered back together in Vienna, Austria, to share about our ministries and the work the Lord had done in and through our lives. On our last night together over 300 of us celebrated with a beautiful meal, and a closing message given by Bud. The food was great, the fellowship rich, and the message second to none.

I learned afresh that nothing compares to the Word of God.

Bud took his place at the podium with his Bible in his hand, smiling from ear to ear, looking around the room at faces whose lives had forever been changed. As he began, the room grew very quiet. With strength and conviction the words spilled from his mouth—familiar words, God's words, each and every word from the book of II Timothy. Bud could have shared anything from his heart that night, and we would have listened. But reciting the memorized words of II Timothy had much greater impact than any words of his own. Etched in my memory is that summer night in Vienna, Austria. I learned afresh that nothing compares to the Word of God.

In Philippians 3:17 Paul urges his readers to follow his example. He repeats the exhortation in Philippians 4:9. In this epistle we clearly see that Paul patterned his life after His Savior, and we do well to follow in his footsteps. Paul's priorities centered on the gospel of Jesus Christ, and his desire and goal were to glorify Him. We find practical, powerful promises with which to fill our minds, and upon which to base our lives. Indeed, as was evidenced in Bud's life, nothing compares to the Word of God.

While you study, ask the Lord to deepen your love for His Word—as Him to give you an insatiable desire to know it like my friend did. Thank Him for the people in your life who point you to Christ, and pray you will be that person for someone else. Remember that the Christian life is all about giving glory and honor to our King!

DAY ONE

☐ Read Philippians

Live in Harmony—Philippians 4:2-3

Paul prays for abounding love, knowledge, and discernment, models, and calls for Christ-centered living. He charges us with unity of heart and singleness of purpose, reminds us of the humility and exaltation of our Savior, and emphasizes our responsibility toward the world. Timothy and Epaphroditus are given as examples of commitment to Paul and ultimately commitment to the Father. Paul warns us against the false believers and calls us to press on toward the goal of the upward call of God in Christ Jesus, giving us a glimpse of what we will be like when Jesus comes again. And concluding his letter, he reminds us once again of the importance of unity of heart, mind, and purpose as we labor together as believers.

1. Read Philippians 4:2-3.

   a. According to Philippians 4:3, what kind of women are Euodia and Syntyche (use Scripture to support your answer)?

2. Euodia and Syntyche are godly women! Paul exhorts them to "live in harmony in the Lord." Another way of phrasing this would be, "be of the same mind." Why is harmonious living sometimes such a challenge?

3. Look back to Philippians 2:1-5. What exhortations apply to situations that are similar to Euodia and Syntyche's conflict?

4.   TRUTH SEARCH:

Study the following principles found in the book of Proverbs. Record what you learn about maintaining harmonius relationships with one another.

Proverbs 12:15

Proverbs 13:10

Proverbs 15:1

Proverbs 16:32

Proverbs 17:14

Proverbs 25:8-10

Reflection

Paul genuinely cares for these two women, as well as Clement and the other fellow workers. He reminds them that all of their names are in the "book of life." As children of God, we all have the assurance of forgiveness and the hope of eternal life, and we share an intimate relationship with our Lord and Savior. We must remember that we are working together in the cause of the gospel—looking ahead to the day of glory. Following the example Jesus Christ set for us is imperative as we serve Him together—united in spirit, intent on one purpose. Check your own heart to be sure you are creating harmony and not dissension in your group or church.

DAY TWO

☐ Read Philippians

Apprehending Our Anxiety—Philippians 4:4-7

Take one look at the headlines of your local paper, or spend one evening watching the local and national news, and you will undoubtedly find yourself feeling anxious. We live in uncertain days, danger looms on the horizon, and it's easy to feel absolutely out of control. Maybe you don't have time to concern yourself with the world's affairs, but you find that you're constantly worried about money, your children's education, your future, the security of your job. There is always something that keeps you from experiencing the peace Jesus promised. This passage is so simple and practical; pray that the Lord will help to make it come alive in your daily experience.

5. a. As you read Philippians today how many times does Paul repeat the word "joy" or "rejoice?"

    b. Why is joy emphasized, and where is true joy found? Use Philippians to support your answer.

6. a. An attitude of joy sets the believer apart from the rest of the world! By looking into the face of Jesus, we find countless reasons to rejoice and be thankful. Make a list of <u>everything</u> you're thankful for, then thank the Lord for everything on your list.

"Let all men know and perceive and recognize your selflessness—your considerateness[sic], your forbearing spirit. The Lord is near—He is coming soon."—Philippians 4:5, *Amplified Bible*

b. What is our motivation for "selfless and considerate living?"

c. How does this attitude differ from that of the world?

7. With joy and the nearness of God as our backdrop, what four instructions does Philippians 4:6 give?

8. The dictionary defines <u>anxiety</u> as, "a state of being uneasy, apprehensive, or worried about what may happen; concern about a possible future event."[1] All of us are prone to anxiety. At one time or another during the past month, week, day, or even hour we have experienced varying degrees of anxiety. Perhaps you interviewed for an important job, your money is tight and rent is due, or you are apprehensive about beginning a new relationship. It is easy to dwell on and worry about things over which we have no control. On an even more regular basis we worry about being late, disappointing someone, trying something new, or having enough money for the parking meter. Jesus knew this and, inspired by the Holy Spirit and punctuated by his own experience, so did Paul. Remarkably, he tells us to worry or be anxious about nothing, and in everything, with thanksgiving, let our requests be known to God. What is the result?

9. Read Philippians 4:7. When we take our worries—all of them—to the Lord, what kind of peace will guard our hearts and our minds?

10. TRUTH SEARCH:

    Compare Philippians 4:6-7 with Matthew 6:25-34.

    a. List all of the things that cause anxiety—notice Matthew 6:32 says that the Gentiles (non-believers) worry about the same things we do.

    b. What things cause you worry and stress?

    c. Why is the Lord Jesus worthy of our trust?

Reflection

I memorized Philippians 4:6-7 a long time ago. Each time I choose to apply this truth to my own worries and woes, I experience the surpassing peace of God guarding my heart and my mind in Christ Jesus. The following is an example of how to apply this truth in your own life no matter the size or weight of your anxiety:

"Lord, thank You for Your Word that is truer than my feelings and my circumstances. Thank You that You tell me to be anxious for NOTHING, but in EVERYTHING, with THANKSGIVING, I am to let my requests be made known to You. I am anxious about my dentist appointment. You know how afraid I am of lying back in that chair, being defenseless against the needles, the drilling, the drooling. I do not want to faint, so I am thanking you for my dentist, my teeth, and the fact that You will be with me during my appointment. I pray You will give my dentist wisdom and gentleness as he works on my teeth. Thank You that Your Word promises me peace—Your peace—which will guard my heart and my mind in Christ."

DAY THREE

☐ Read Philippians

@ DIGGING DEEPER

There is nothing like the Word of God. Nothing. Today we're going to spend time looking at the benefits of God's Word, the power of God's Word, and the importance of renewing our minds. Pray that your heart will be teachable and encouraged as you look at these amazing truths.

11. The following is a list of a few passages that describe both the importance of the Word of God and the benefit of spending time reading and studying it. Meditate on the verses and write down your discoveries:

Deuteronomy 6:4-9

Proverbs 16:20

Proverbs 30:5

Ecclesiastes 12:12-13

12. Look up the following passages and record what you learn about the power of God's Word: Psalm 19:7-11; Romans 10:17; II Timothy 3:16; Hebrews 4:12.

13. Read the subsequent verses and explain why we need to continually renew our minds:
Romans 12:2

II Corinthians 9:5

Ephesians 4:20-24

13. What have you learned about the Word of God and the act of renewing your mind that is practical to your life right now, and why?

Reflection

The Lord has proven to me over and over again that when I run to His Word I will always find the comfort and the answers that I need for any given situation. It's not easy to do. Every time I wrestle with something, I am tempted to try to take care of it on my own or to "process" with a friend; however, when I resist that urge and open my Bible instead, I find my needs are met in a much greater way. Resist the urge to call your friends or to cry on someone's shoulder when you're lonely, in need of comfort, looking for wisdom, or when you need a listening ear. Sit at the feet of Jesus, open up His Word—His love-letter to you. Within its pages you will find treasures that will meet your needs in much deeper ways than you ever thought possible.

DAY FOUR

☐ Read Philippians

In Pursuit of Excellence—Philippians 4:9

Anxiety, worry, stress, and depression begin pounding on the door of our thoughts, and before we know it they're making themselves at home in the living-room of our minds. Soon they've taken up residence—eating, drinking, pestering, bothering at all hours of the day and night. The voice of anxiety screams. Worry frets. Meanwhile stress paces back and forth tormenting our thoughts, and eventually bursting out in our words and through our actions. Philippians 4:6-7 provides step by step instructions for dealing with all our anxieties. Philippians 4:8 gives us the key to ongoing victory: mind-renewal.

15. Record Philippians 4:8. What is the main source of the things that are true, honorable, right, pure, lovely, of good repute, excellent, and worthy of praise?

16. What does it mean to "let your mind dwell on these things?"

17. According to Philippians 4:9, what is the result of "practicing these things?"

Reflection

Let me exhort you to take to heart Philippians 4:8-9. When you choose to dwell on the things listed in these verses, you are choosing to think on Jesus Christ. Allowing your mind to drift to places it does not belong comes too naturally. It is easy to allow lustful, vengeful, hateful, and sorrowful thoughts to enter the doorway of your mind. Once they cross the threshold it is not long before they are abiding, and before you know it, the world, the flesh, and the devil smother anything that resembles joy or excellence. When those thoughts knock on the door of your heart and mind—and they surely will—make a choice to replace them with the truth of God's Word.

DAY FIVE

☐ Read Philippians

Real Life

18. a. My husband once told me, "Don't let Satan rob you of your joy." What tends to rob you of your joy in Christ, and why?

   b. Based upon your study, what will help you keep an attitude of joy?

19. a. How do you react to life when you are anxious and worried? Think about how you handle stress and pressure. Do you tend to withdraw or become fierce?

   b. Have you put Philippians 4:6-8 into practice? What was the result?

c. What should you do if you take these verses seriously, but the anxiety remains?

20. Describe a time in your life when you experienced peace that was utterly unexplainable.

Reflection

My friend Bud Hinkson went home to the Lord several years ago, but his example of a man who loved the Lord and His Word lives on in my life and the lives of countless others. From conversations I had with his family and close friends, I am quite certain he had memorized more Scripture than anyone I have ever met, and it was obvious. Bud's joyous enthusiasm was undeniably an overflow of his love for the Savior and his knowledge of the Word. It was contagious.

Largely due to Bud's example, I have worked at memorizing various passages in the Bible. I have found that the Lord will often bring specific verses and passages to mind at exactly the right moment—especially when those emotions I mentioned earlier in the lesson come knocking at the door of my mind. As I get older I find that memorization takes a lot longer than it used to, but I'm determined to continue because it's too easy for me to forget what is true and believe what is not! Let me encourage you, whether you're good at it or not, make Scripture memory a regular part of your devotional life.

Copy Philippians 4:2-9 in the back of your book or in your journal.

1 Webster

"Not that I speak from want, for
I have learned to be content in
whatever circumstances I am."

Philippians 4:11

Transformed Contentment

Philippians 4:10-23

Living passionately for Christ, as we've learned through our study, begins with our hearts set upon Jesus Christ—our Lord and our Savior. He began a good work in the hearts and lives of the Philippians some 2000 years ago and continues to do the same in our lives today. As we've discovered, living passionately for Christ is defined by our commitment to the Savior, our sacrificial love for one another, our Christ-centered priorities, living in light of eternity, and seeking the peace that surpasses comprehension. Ultimately it's a matter of the heart. As we finish our study of Philippians chapter 4, we'll look once again at the source of passionate living—Jesus Christ. We will consider the "secret" to contentment, and the source of our power and our provision.

Ultimately it's a matter of the heart.

As you begin, pray and ask the Lord to drive home the truth of His Word. Beg Him to strengthen you with His resurrection power that you may finish the course triumphant, ready to receive your eternal reward, transformed by His glory.

DAY ONE

☐ Read Philippians

Paul's Secret—Philippians 4:10-18

Paul concludes his letter to the Philippians by encouraging them for their participation in God's provision for his life. Not only had they participated in the gospel, as he mentioned in chapter one, but they also participated in providing for Paul materially. I love how Paul thanks them—recognizing their generosity—and yet gives God the glory as the true Provider.

1. Read Philippians 4:10-18. Look carefully at the context. How does Paul describe the Philippians' participation in his ministry?

2. a. How does Paul describe their gift in Philippians 4:18 and why?

   b According to Philippians 4:17 Paul isn't seeking the money for his own benefit but recognizes the blessing this church will receive as a result of their sacrificial gift. In what ways have you experienced the blessing of giving of your time or talents sacrificially?

3. TRUTH SEARCH:

    a. Look at the following passages and describe some of Paul's circumstances: II Corinthians 6:1-10 and II Corinthians 12:7-10, and look back to Philippians 1:12-21.

    b. Compare Philippians 4:11-13 with the previous passages. What is the secret of Paul's contentment?

4. Think about your own life and the areas that challenge your happiness—money, possessions, relationships, health. Based upon all that we've learned in our study, how is contentment possible no matter the circumstance? Use this question as an opportunity to review the previous three chapters.

5. We've discussed the strength of having an eternal perspective throughout our study. How does having such a perspective help us in the area of contentment?

Reflection

Time and again in Philippians we are exhorted by Paul's words (inspired by God) and his example (a result of God's strength) to remember Jesus Christ. I cannot emphasize enough our need to spend serious time reading our Bibles and pouring out our hearts to the Lord. The battle for victorious Christian living is fought and won at the feet of our Savior.

DAY TWO

☐ Read Philippians

Our Provider—Philippians 4:19-23

God is the source of our salvation, our transformation, our purpose, our love, our hope, and our provision. As we look at these final verses, thank the Lord for all that He has given you spiritually, materially, mentally, and emotionally. He is our Provider.

6. Philippians 4:19 holds what promise?

7. Review Philippians again, and this time look at all of the specific ways the Lord provided for Paul and for us—His example, His power, His strength, etc.

8. For what purpose does God provide all of our needs according to Philippians 4:20?

9. Remember that Paul was a prisoner in Rome and yet the gospel was not imprisoned.

    a. Who are among the believers who sent greetings to Philippi?

    b. Compare this with Philippians 1:12-17. What does this tell you about God's sovereign and eternal purposes?

Reflection

Make a list of all of your current needs—material as well as emotional, physical, and mental. Pour out your heart to the Lord. Confess your inadequacies, your fears, your wants and your desires. Claim the promise found in Philippians 4:19—write it over the top of your list—and trust Him to be true to His Word.

Keep track of His provision. Record how He meets your needs and fulfills His purposes in your life.

DAY THREE

☐ Read Philippians

@ DIGGING DEEPER

The Bible has a great deal to say about sacrifice. In fact, the Old Testament law and covenant centered around sacrifice, especially the blood sacrifice that atoned for sins once a year. This was a picture of the coming of God's ultimate sacrifice—that of His only begotten Son. In Philippians chapter two we studied the impact of the Lord's sacrifice on the cross on our behalf. In addition we considered the result of His sacrifice in our lives personally—the transformation of our hearts, our purpose, relationships, and perspective—along with the blessings that flow through our lives as a result of Christ emptying Himself of His deity and dying for our sins. What does sacrificial living mean for us as we live for Him? Romans 12:1 says we're to present ourselves as a "living and holy sacrifice" to God. Paul commended the Philippians for their "acceptable sacrifice" which was "well-pleasing" to God. Study the following verses and discover what living sacrificially means in your life.

10. Read Psalm 51 and record what you discover about the heart of the Psalmist.

11. Look at each section and record the requests the Psalmist makes of the Lord.
      Psalm 51:1-4

      Psalm 51:5-9

      Psalm 51:10-13

      Psalm 51:14-17

12. a. After all is said and done, what does the Psalmist discover pleases the Lord in Psalm 51:17?

LESSON 9: TRANSFORMED CONTENTMENT ❖ 129

b. Compare this with Micah 6:8 and Romans 12:1-2 and describe what being wholly devoted to Christ really means.

Reflection

Is your life a fragrant aroma, a pleasing sacrifice to God? Is He at the center of your heart? If He is, praise Him for giving you the strength and power to live for Him. If He is not—stop here and walk through Psalm 51 with Him. Give Him all of the things that are keeping you from pure and holy devotion to Him. Ask Him to break your heart and humble your soul that you might live passionately for Him.

DAY FOUR

☐ Read Philippians

Cultivating Contentment—Philippians 4:19

Why is it that we struggle so much with contentment? It seems that no matter what we have we want more, then once we get more we're still unhappy. It can be a vicious cycle if we're not careful and Christ-centered. As we've learned, if we seek to be satisfied by the world we'll never be happy, but if we live wholeheartedly for Christ we will be satisfied…it's a promise.

13. Where are you on the pathway to contentment? Consider those things that challenge your contentment and tempt you to bemoan your circumstances.

14. Philippians 4:19 says that "God will supply all of our needs according to His riches in glory." For what needs are you currently trusting the Lord, and how does this powerful verse encourage you? Thank Him by faith for being true to His Word (remember this promise applies to all your needs from finding a job or a spouse, to relief from an affliction).

15. Perhaps some of the "needs" in your life aren't really necessary. Ask the Lord to be your sole satisfaction—to meet your needs both materially and emotionally.

Reflection

I recently told my husband that I am learning to be content with much. "How in the world is it possible to have to *learn* to be content with much?" I've wondered with the Lord. We used to be on the mission field, living in a one-room flat in post-communist Russia. Sometimes we weren't sure if we'd have hot water or heat, and there were days when finding food was a challenge. I had to learn to be content then too—with little. It's easy to want to be somewhere other than where the Lord has us—that's the challenge of contentment. He wants to be and needs to be—must be—our sole-satisfaction. By faith we need to trust Him daily—that we're right where He wants us to be. Psalm 25:10 says, "All the paths of the Lord are lovingkindness and truth to those who keep His covenant and testimonies." Are you content to be on the path where the Lord has placed you on today? Ask Him to help you to rejoice and be glad—right where He has you.

DAY FIVE

☐ Read Philippians

Real Life

Philippians is a rich book of Scripture—full of motivating truths, powerful promises, and a picture of Jesus Christ our Savior that is humbling and challenging. All four chapters give us reason for pursuing an intimate relationship with the One who gave His life for us, who is transforming us, who is living in and through us, and who is waiting for us in heaven. As you conclude your study prayerfully consider the following questions, and finish by worshipping your Lord and Savior.

16. Read Philippians aloud. Stop and praise the Lord for the truths that have ministered to or motivated you to change, or to trust God in a new way during your study of this chapter.

17. How does the promise of Philippians 4:13 encourage you personally and how will you apply it to your life this week?

Reflection

How are you doing personally in the area of contentment? If you find that you're regularly unhappy with your life make it a practice to "rejoice in the Lord" for every single situation in your life—no matter how difficult or trying. Review your word study on joy from lesson three, or do it now. Look to Jesus and His Word to meet your needs.

"Only one life, soon it shall
pass, only what's done for Christ
shall last."

Jim Elliot

Live Passionately for Christ

If you're like me you've asked yourself, "What does it look like to live passionately for Christ, to live in light of eternity if I'm raising children, building a home, or landscaping my yard? What if I'm developing a new relationship, pursuing a career, serving on the mission field, going to school, or making my bed? What if I'm giving constant care to someone who is ill, am completely bedridden, or am too old? And, better yet, how do I maintain zealous living for a lifetime?" Paul answered these questions while sitting in a prison cell: "whether by life or by death, Christ be exalted." All the way to the cross Jesus set an example for us follow with His heart attitude and His actions, emphasizing with His words: "I always do the things that are pleasing to Him" (John 8:29). The higher value we place on knowing Jesus Christ our Lord, the greater will our desire be to honor Him with every ounce of our being. The more intimately we know our Savior, the better we will understand His infinite love, grace, and forgiveness. When our fervor wanes and we lose heart, I'm certain that if we keep our eyes fixed on Jesus, His strength will be perfected in our weaknesses (II Corinthians 12:9), and His divine power will provide for us everything we need pertaining to life and godliness (II Peter 1:3). How do I know? The Bible tells me so!

How do I maintain zealous living for a lifetime?

The goals of our study of Philippians have been to "ascertain the source of and the reason for passionate, Christ-centered living" and to "discover what sets us apart, how to make an impact on the world, and stretch the limits of our faith." Have we accomplished these goals? Lesson Ten will help you answer this question for yourself and take the next step in your life with Christ. As you begin, pray that the Lord will use this time to show you what you've learned, to encourage you in your growth, and to motivate you to apply these truths to a lifetime of passionate living.

LIVING PASSIONATELY

1. a. Describe what "living passionately for Christ" meant to you before you began your study of Philippians.

    b. How has your description changed over the course of the past nine lessons?

2. Based upon what you've learned, what sets us as believers apart from the world around us (use Scripture to support your answer)?

3. In what ways have the limits of your faith been stretched as you've studied Philippians? Consider such questions as these: How have I grown closer to the Lord? Has He answered specific prayers or touched my heart in a specific way? Has He used me to share the gospel with someone? How has He changed my values?

4. It is clear that a transformation takes place in our lives at the very moment of salvation and continues throughout our lives with Christ. Each chapter of this study guide focused on a particular aspect of transformation. Review each lesson and consider the ways in which the Lord has caused a *metamorphosis*—"a complete change of character, appearance, or condition," in each of the following areas of your life:

   a. your passion

   b. your confidence

   c. your purpose

   d. your relationships

   e. your way of life

   f. your heart

   g. your goals

   h. your mind

   i. your contentment

5. What truths from your study of Philippians will you impart to another believer, and why?

6. What steps are you taking *today* to ensure Christ-centered passion for the rest of your life?

Reflection

It is my prayer that your study of Philippians has enhanced your relationship with the Lord in such a way that you'll be compelled to pursue Him with a fresh zeal and a renewed confidence. I hope that, with an eye toward eternity, you will find new opportunities to share the gospel, and circumstances in which to encourage other believers. I pray you've experienced victory over sin, newfound and lasting contentment, and a joy and confidence that will thrive wherever the Lord takes you. Live passionately for Christ—to Him be the glory forever and ever, Amen!

Copy Philippians 4:10-23 in the back of your book or in your journal.

BIBLIOGRAPHY

Henry and Scott. Commentary on the Holy Bible, Volume 6, Romans to Revelation.
    Grand Rapids: Baker House.

Ironside, H.A. Notes on Philippians.
    Neptune, Loizeau Brothers, 1979.

MacArthur, John   The MacArthur New Testament Commentary Philippians.
    Chicago: Moody Press, 2001.

McCutcheon, Mark. Roget's Super Thesaurus, Second Edition.
    Cincinnati: Writer's Digest Books, 1998.

Webster's New World Dictionary of the American Language, Second College Edition.
    New York and Cleveland: The World Publishing Company, 1970.

NOTES

NOTES

NOTES

NOTES

NOTES

NOTES

NOTES

NOTES

NOTES

Made in the USA
Lexington, KY
11 October 2012